THE ROADS FROM THE ISLES

LOCH MAREE

From the Poolewe—Kinlochewe track near
Ardlair, with a distant view of the massive
sandstone mountains of Torridon across the loch.

THE ROADS FROM THE ISLES

A
STUDY OF THE
NORTH-WEST HIGHLAND TRACKS

D. D. C. POCHIN MOULD

OLIVER AND BOYD
EDINBURGH: TWEEDDALE COURT
LONDON: 98 GREAT RUSSELL STREET, W.C.

FIRST PUBLISHED . . . 1950

PRINTED IN GREAT BRITAIN BY
ROBERT CUNNINGHAM AND SONS LTD., ALVA
FOR OLIVER AND BOYD LTD., EDINBURGH

FOREWORD

I have attempted in this book to tell the story of some of the old roads through the North-West Highlands, of the places they linked, of the people who used them and the way in which geology and geography have determined their routes. For the most part, this is the story of roads from the Isles, and following these roads from the hilltops along the way, there is as background the Minch and the Hebrides.

This book, too, is a confession of faith in the Highlands. For, if I have written of the past, it is not because I think there is no future for the Highlands. The cattle no longer walk the drove roads south; but the hills can still rear them, as recent experiments prove. The power cables are stringing across the hills beside the ancient rights of way, and the lights are going on in remote clachans. Of themselves, not hydro-electric schemes, nor forestry, nor cattle ranching, can save the Highlands, but they are the tools with which we may, if we have enough courage, build the future.

So then, when one halts at the top of the pass, looking down on that almost incredible blend of rock and water and forest that is the beauty of the North, it is to the future that one's thoughts turn. In the twists of the old road below, is the story of the past, but it is to the making of the new, streamlined road, that is the promise of the future, to which we must turn our hands.

D. D. C. Pochin Mould

Inchnacardoch,
Fort Augustus

CONTENTS

PART I
THE ROAD IN THE HIGHLANDS

PART II
THE GREAT ROAD TO THE SOUTH

PART III
THE ROAD OF THE DEAD

PART IV
THE CATTLE ROAD FROM THE ISLES

PART V
THE ROAD THE SOLDIERS MADE

PART VI
THE VERY OLD ROAD FROM THE WEST
TO THE EAST

PART VII
THE ROAD BY THE SEA

PART VIII
THE ROAD ACROSS THE NORTH OF SCOTLAND

PART IX
THE FAR NORTH

PART X
THE ROAD FROM THE ISLES

ILLUSTRATIONS

I

THE ROAD IN THE HIGHLANDS

CHAPTER I

THE ROAD

THE Road is a strange man-made magic. For only men make roads; beasts have but the faint trails down to the drinking-places and the fresh grass in the valleys. And the courses of birds and of aeroplanes, of fish and ships, are lost even as they are made. Only on land, only by man's making, runs the wizardry of the road: the firm, sure track joining town with town, port with port, industry with demand.

The Road is a curious link. For it links not only in space but in time, joining not only one place with another, but linking also the common experience of all men who have gone that way from century to century. Our motors run close on the heels of medieval pilgrims and Roman legionaries.

This book is the story of some few roads in the North-West Highlands of Scotland, that lonely and beautiful country between the rift of the Great Glen and the swift currents of Cape Wrath. It is not the story of all the roads in that country, nor of all the grass-grown rights-of-way, for such a book would be of many volumes. It is the story of the old grass-grown way from the port of Poolewe to the South country; of the pass across Drum Alban that the Celtic saints followed; of the road that Island cattle took to the southern markets; of the way the English soldiers made to Glenelg; and of lonely tracks that link croft with croft along the Atlantic's shores and solitary paths in the desolate northern hills.

3

General George Wade was the first man to construct a system of roads in the Highlands. In England and the south of Scotland, the road-maker's heritage is far older, going back to the Roman roads, whose lines still guide the course of our modern motor roads.

But the Romans failed to conquer Scotland. They held uneasy rule between Hadrian's Wall and the Antonine line between Forth and Clyde, long enough to build roads there, the course of which some of the Border roads still follow. But north of the Highland line, the Romans only carried out costly raids in force, and north of the Great Glen they never went at all. The Highland roads, unlike those of the South, never had the pattern of Roman straight lines for a basis of development.

When the first settlers landed on the Highland shores, it was a strange wild country that they found. Densely wooded, it was covered with a vast growth of pine and oak and birch, the last remnants of which still skirt the Cairngorms or survive in dwindling patches in the north. Out of the dark woods, where lurked not only deer but also packs of wolves and herds of wild pigs, rose the craggy summits of the mountains, mountains that seemed to be the home of strange and evil spirits, tremendous and mysterious. The ground was wetter than it is to-day, and there were great bogs that sucked in man and beast. To-day, it is hard to realise that hardly any Highland hillside is not criss-crossed with man-cut drainage ditches, made for the management of sheep walks and deer forests. Once the water which runs down these drains, stood in vast moor bogs.

Then too, the great mountain range of Drum Alban (the ridge of Alba or Scotland), which runs from Loch Lomond, up the western seaboard to Cape Wrath, at first formed an impenetrable barrier between the men who settled upon the west and the men who settled upon the east coast.

Forest clearance could only begin with the coming of cheap

and abundant iron tools—with the beginning of the Iron Age. It went on, without much thought of replanting, until the beginning of the eighteenth century, when men began to realise that the country would be left quite treeless unless plantations were begun.

Woodland was cleared for many reasons. To bring more land under arable cultivation; to make charcoal to smelt iron; for building materials; to clear up the lurking places of robbers and wolves. Wolves remained a danger to Highland travellers up to the middle of the seventeenth century.

The Romans realised the strategic value of dense woodland to the native population. When, at the end of the third century, the Emperor Severus fought his way as far north as the Moray Firth—the farthest point the Romans reached on land —he not only built roads but cleared woodland.

Then, too, forest fires must have destroyed much of the ancient woodland. Some would be accidental; but what more satisfying than after a successful raid to see all your neighbour's country lit with leaping flames?

There are certain lines between given centres that a road or track, which grows naturally as did the Highland tracks (tracks they were and tracks many of them remain to this day), will take.

In a mountainous country it will avoid the peaks. This is in marked distinction to the South Country ridgeways of the Downs, where the ancient roads ran on the tops of the downland ridges, keeping clear of the marsh and wood in the valleys below. In Scotland, the roads follow the valleys and usually manage to get across watersheds by crossing the low cols at the head of the valleys: steep hills are rather notably absent on Scottish main roads to-day.

The tracks thus follow the through valleys, in which they will pick out the dry ground and seek for moderately safe places to cross streams, for bridges were few and, in the North and

West, almost non-existent until quite recent times. There is a marked difference in the places where a bridged and non-bridged road will choose to cross a stream. For a safe ford, one picks a gravelly bottom with no large boulders beside which deep pools can be hollowed out, where the stream broadens and shallows and where there are no dangerous currents or rapids. For a bridge crossing, and one has only to think of a number of Wade's little bridges, the road will seek the narrowest part of the river to span, at a place where a firm foundation can be got on each side to build on, and if possible, where stone for building is available nearby. A rocky gorge, narrow, violent with waterfalls and deep pools, quite unfordable, may be an ideal site for a single span, stone bridge.

Then too, water supplies are important. It is notable that the Highland drove roads nearly always follow lines along which springs of pure water are available. The Highlanders not only endowed their springs with various sprites and fancies, but were very particular about drinking water. They would go a long distance to a favourite spring rather than drink from a stream close by.

The old Highland population was hardly road-minded. There was, after all, security in being quite inaccessible. Still, there was a considerable come and go through the Highlands in the old times, not only of raiding clans but of commerce. Sea transport was, as it must always be in a mountainous, fiord-cut land, extremely important. Clan Campbell do not show the Galley of Lorne on their banner for nothing. There are still little West Coast communities who are dependent on the sea and have no road linking them with the rest of the world.

It was during the latter half of the seventeenth century that the great trade in the black cattle which the Highlands and Islands reared, became important. The drovers took the cattle slowly southward over the wide drove roads or cattle raikes, along which the cattle fed and improved as they travelled.

When General Wade began his roads in the early 1720's, he had these cattle raikes as a guide on which to base the course of his military roads.

Wade's military roads came no farther north than the line down the Great Glen, which linked Fort George (Inverness), Fort Augustus and Fort William. He did not continue them north of the Great Glen.

Then came the flare-up of the '45 and, after it, a fresh spurt of military road-making. These roads were called the New Roads in distinction to the Old Roads of General Wade. Only two of them were made north of the Great Glen: one from Fort Augustus to the barracks at Bernera near Glenelg, and the other from Contin to the west coast port of Poolewe. The new military roads were finally handed over to the Parliamentary Commissioners by the military authorities in 1814, under the Highland Roads and Bridges Act. Because these roads were under official control did not mean that they were good roads. At the end of the eighteenth century, the Countess of Seaforth determined to drive her coach over the Contin-Poolewe road, from which last place she was to embark for Lewis. By the time she had got as far as Loch Achanault, not half-way, the coach was so wrecked as to be past all repair.

Most of the traffic on the roads went on foot or on pack pony. The ponies carried two panniers or creels, which held 256 lbs. or 2 bolls of meal. When the military roads were first made and surfaced, the Highlanders grumbled because the stones hurt their bare or thin-shod feet and were useless to their unshod ponies. They also resented the erection of milestones recording "English" miles and pulled them up over night, because they would not have the foreign measure imposed on them.

The Highland method of computing miles is well described by the minister of Applecross in the *Statistical Account of*

B

Scotland (1792).* He writes of his parish that there was "neither public road nor bridge from one extremity of it to the other. . . . The foot traveller is guided, according to the season of the year, what course to take, over rugged hills, rapid waters, and deep and marshy burns. Besides here, as in all the adjoining parishes and Western Isles, the computation of miles is merely arbitrary, always terminated by a burn, cairn, well, or some such accidental mark, which renders them so remarkably unequal that it is impossible to reduce any given number of these imaginary miles to a regular computation."

Still, properly made roads eventually came to the North-West Highlands, partly by statute labour and partly by the works of the various proprietors. Some were built to provide employment in the potato famine, which began in 1846. But they were not very good roads, narrow and tricky to drive a car over, until the reconstruction works of the 1930's began. And even the reconstructed roads are mostly for single-line traffic only, with passing places marked by black and white painted poles.

If you mark the present North-West Highland roads upon a map, and then the lines of all the important cross-country tracks and rights-of-way, a startling fact emerges. Whereas in densely populated England, there would be many more new roads than old; here in the north, there are more old tracks than existing roads. And the tracks that are out of use are often routes that would still be useful to-day and would cut off many miles of cross-country journeying. Whereby hangs the sorry tale of Highland depopulation.

The clan system died for Prince Charles in 1746. The

* Dates of the Statistical Accounts. In the case of material quoted from the old Statistical Account, the date given is that of the publication of the volume in which the particular reference occurs. In the case of the New Statistical Account, the date quoted is that given against the parish referred to—that is the date when the particular minister wrote it, not the date of publication of the whole series (1840).

glens were then populated with small, self-contained and moderately well content units who lived simply on the land. Their principal stock was black cattle, with a few small and rather delicate sheep, and sturdy little ponies. In the summer, the womenfolk and boys took the cattle up to the hill pastures where they lived in the summer shielings, tending the herds and making butter and cheeses. Meantime, the men worked on the arable land in the valleys. Along the coast, there was a considerable trade in catching and exporting fish.

To the landowners, now greatly impoverished, came, toward the end of the eighteenth century, the vision of the Golden Fleece. The hill pastures were found to be ideal for the hardy black-faced and Cheviot sheep. But you cannot eat your pasture twice over. The Highland clearances began, and the black cattle economy with its well-populated glens, gave place to the sheep economy with a single shepherd to many hundreds of acres. The evicted tenants either drifted south or emigrated to the Americas.

> From the lone shieling of the misty island
> Mountains divide us, and the waste of seas—
> Yet still the blood is strong, the heart is Highland,
> And we in dreams behold the Hebrides.

A little later on there were fresh evictions; for the Highland crofter has only very recently gained any security of tenure of his holding; this time in the name of the Deer.

Even at the peak of the boom in sheep and deer, astute men, saw that it might not last for ever and that always thriving communities of men and a balanced agriculture were more profitable in the long run than the sterile wastes of the deer forests and the deserts of the sheep walks.

Once started, depopulation goes on of itself, for the diminished townships have less and less to offer to their youth. In Wester Ross, from 1881 to 1931, after the time of the "clearances", a survey of the population trends shows that (with the exception of Lochalsh) all the parishes have lost a quarter to half of their people. In the same fifty years, the population of Scotland as a whole grew by a third.

So it has come about that the Scottish Highlands are lonely and marked with the ruins of houses. It is this generation's business to turn back the drift from the Highlands, and prove that there is a worth-while life to be lived in one of the most tremendous settings in which man has ever dwelt.

II

THE GREAT ROAD TO THE SOUTH

CHAPTER II

THE FORGE OF SCOTLAND

THE right-of-way from Poolewe on the West Coast, to Fort Augustus in the Great Glen, and on to the southward by the Corrieyairack Pass, is surely one of this island's great cross-country routes. From the West Highland beaches in sight of the Isles, past the long, lovely stretch of Loch Maree and the fantastic hills of Torridon sandstone, across the desolate moors to Loch Monar, through the three glens that are claimed as Scotland's loveliest, Strathfarrar, Cannich, Affric, through the woods to Fort Augustus in sight of Ben Nevis, and then away and up over Wade's route across Corrieyairack—once the highest road in Britain.

Poolewe was once an important port. It handled the traffic for Lewis. To it, Prince Charles, during his wanderings, sent messengers to try and contact a French vessel which he hoped might take him out of Scotland. In later times, the Lewis mail boat left from Poolewe. Various foreign boats also put in here, perhaps not always with lawful cargo! In World War II, Poolewe again saw important shipping.

The present main road to Poolewe goes upon the south-west shore of Loch Maree to Gairloch and then over the hill by Loch Tollie to Poolewe. This route is a fairly modern road, mostly built during the potato famine as a relief measure. There was no bridge over the river Ewe at Poolewe until about 1836. The old road did not cross the Ewe, but went round by Loch Kernsary, dropping down to the north-east shore of Loch Maree at Ardlair. It followed Loch Maree side to the head of the loch, forded the Kinlochewe river near the present village of Kinlochewe, and crossed the hills to the Coulin Pass.

Because Poolewe was an important port of call, it formed the terminus of one of the only two military roads made north of the Great Glen. This military road seems also to have run along the old track north-east of Loch Maree. From Kinlochewe, it went up Glen Docherty and into the Achnasheen-Dingwall through valley, to Contin. But little work seems to have been done on this military road. It is mentioned amongst those being carried on in 1761: it appears in the detailed estimates for the military roads for the years 1770-1780. There was a party of 25 privates, 2 sergeants and 2 corporals kept at work on the route. But it was on this road, that the Countess of Seaforth wrecked her coach in trying to drive to Poolewe, and most of the traffic must have been on foot or pack horse.

Then too, on Loch Maree, were founded the first ironworks of which Scotland has any historic records, and on the hills are the remains of far older furnaces. Here, too, you may walk upon the ancient land surface formed in pre-Torridonian times, and explore ancient valleys into which the Torridonian sands and gravels were washed. Or visit the island where St. Maelrubha founded a little church, and where his memory became hoplessly confused with a well to cure insanity and an ancient rite of sacrificing bulls.

The gorse was a blaze of gold when I halted the car at Poolewe and turned up the old track at Sron Dubh. Elsewhere the gorse was burned brown by the 1947 frosts, but here, in the sheltered bay, it was untouched. The tide was running out, and the smell of hot tangle mingled with that of the gorse. At first, the way ran through thickets of gorse: gorse that rose seven or eight feet high, with every spike a torch of great golden, honey-scented flowers. So thick were the flowers that I could handle the spikes without feeling the prickles underneath. Beyond the gorse, the way went onto a boggy stretch and was almost lost to sight. On this flat between the track and Poolewe, there was held, until about 1720, a great fair. It was called the Feill Iudha, or ewe market. The Lewis men used to come regularly, and the fair came to an end after many of them were drowned in the Minch on their return journey. They used to make the rough crossing in open boats.

As I picked a way over the moor, the track became more distinct, and I came down to the edge of Loch Kernsary. Loch Kernsary is an irregularly-shaped loch, cradled amongst brown moorland, At its head, the few houses of Kernsary form a green, tree-fringed oasis. Ahead, rise the sheer crags of Beinn Airidh Charr (2,593 ft.). This great mountain is made up of Lewisian rocks. It lies between Loch Maree and Fionn Loch, and rises in great crags above the latter, presenting more gradual slopes to Loch Maree. From the foot of Loch Kernsary, Fionn Loch itself cannot be seen, but the Airidh Charr crags can be, as they rise steeply from its hollow. Turning rightwards the eye ranges across the deep hollow of Loch Maree to the fantastic skyline of the mountains of Torridon sandstone, which lie between Loch Maree and the coast. Strange, wall-like peaks they are; often capped by the creamy-white Cambrian quartzites; the line of junction running like a knife-cut below the summit of the hill.

Closer at hand, on Loch Kernsary itself, is a little round island of stones, with a few trees upon it. It is an artificial island; one of the Highland crannogs or lake dwellings. These dwellings may have been very useful places of residence when wolves and wild cattle roamed the hills; though, as they are small and could not hold many people, it seems doubtful if they would be much use against human attackers in any strength.

The crannog on Loch Treig, which was excavated, was most elaborately built of stones and timber. It is somewhat of a problem how the building was done in deepish water in a loch. In Loch Treig, it is thought the water could have been dammed up temporarily, but I doubt that this could be done in most crannog sites—Kernsary for example.

Along the side of Loch Kernsary, I found an interesting piece of track. At one point, the trodden way goes along a six-inch wide notch on an ice-smoothed rock. Hardly a route for wheeled vehicles!

The houses at Kernsary, naturally, do not use this route, but the good private motor road made from Poolewe and Inveran on the River Ewe, to Fionn Loch. The old track crosses this road and makes up the little valley of the burn from Loch Tholldhoire. The loch itself is out of sight behind a low ridge. The track is rough going, as one climbs gently up on to the ridge above Loch Maree. Part consists of large boulders lying in wet peat. It goes below a conical red boulder which stands on the moorland; another track runs above this boulder. It is easy to turn onto this track, instead of the right-of-way to Kernsary, when one walks back from Ardlair. The other track goes down to the Fionn Loch—Poolewe private road, which it joins at Loch an Doire Ghairbh.

As soon as the ridge is gained, Loch Maree lies below one, with its cluster of heavily wooded islands. The hollow of the loch, which actually extends beyond the present end of the loch below Kinlochewe, and up into Glen Docherty, has been determined by a great fault or breakage line in the rocks. This line of weakness is a very ancient one and dates back to pre-Torridonian times. The big fault has been traced from Camas Mor on the coast just east of Rudh'Re to Poolewe; then along the River Ewe to Loch Maree. At Ardlair, it leaves the loch for a short length and runs along the base of the crags of Creag Tharbh. Then it re-enters the loch, extends up

Glen Docherty, and then cross-country to Loch Beannachan in the River Meig basin.

This big fault has an important effect on another fault, called the Fasagh fault. This second fault which has determined the valley of the Abhainn an Fhasaigh, has been shifted horizontally by the Loch Maree fault, which cuts it. Thus the continuation of the Fasagh line of faulting on the other side of Loch Maree from Fasagh is not opposite that point, but has been shifted three miles to the west, where it is found in Glen Grudie.

Loch Maree is rich in islands. There is a property of lakes called their insulosity, which is the ratio of the area of the islands in the lake to the area of water. In Loch Maree, this ratio is 0.09, which is greater than that of any other large lake in Britain (Loch Lomond is 0.08). But it is exceeded by a small loch in Assynt, Loch Crocach, which has an insulosity of 0.091.

The islands of Loch Maree cannot be counted, because when the water is low, many of them are linked above water by land. When the water rises, the links are cut, and the number of islands correspondingly increases. The largest island, Eilean Subhainn, has a loch among its trees. This loch, whose surface is above the level of the water in Loch Maree is 64 feet deep: that is, its deepest level is 30 feet below the level of Loch Maree, When the Bathymetrical Survey was being made of the Scottish fresh water lochs, a boat could not be got on this little loch; so a member of the survey, Mr. Garrett, took the soundings whilst swimming about in the water.

The islands have been used as strongholds in the old times, and for illicit distillation in more recent days. The story of the sacred Isle Maree is better left to form a part of that of the Applecross roads, to which it properly belongs.

Ardlair, where a mansion house stands in a green oasis, has

made up the road in its immediate precincts. Its contact with the outer world, like that of Letterewe farther on, is by boat across Loch Maree. One gets on the good section of road as one comes over the ridge and begins to descend to Loch Maree through the birch wood called Am Fridh Dorcha (the dark wood). Am Fridh Dorcha in the spring is all spread with primroses. Below the shimmering green leaves of the birches and their silvery boles is spread a thick carpet of yellow primroses, which lies even under all the trees. The air is heavy with their scent; one looks down the steep slope on to the mass of flowers, which seem to fill the woodland with a pale golden light.

Between Ardlair and the houses at Letterewe rises the great, tree-hung crag of Creag Tharbh. The name means the Bull Crag, whilst Ardlair is the Mare's Height; both names are said to be derived from the beast-like shapes of rocks fallen from the crag.

The Bull Rock section of the right-of-way is virtually a case of cunning rock climbing between rocks and trees. There is no proper path, the old path never was good and is mostly lost. In following the route from Poolewe to Kinlochewe (about 20 miles), allowance should be made for the facts that most of the way is roughish going; and that the Creag Tharbh is crag-side scrambling.

The ash trees at Ardlair are said to be the descendants of trees planted to provide wood for bows. There were some very famous archers at Gairloch, when the bow was an offensive weapon, of whom a number of stories are told.

Farther along the route, opposite Isle Maree is a hole called the Uamh an Oir, or cave of gold. It is a short day level, excavated by some enterprising person looking for precious metals. The *New Statistical Account* (1836) relates that silver was sought on the sides of Loch Maree. However, neither gold nor silver ever appear to have been found.

Letterewe is another green oasis of trees and fields, a stretch of yellow gorse and a lodge and cottages. The road is again better in the neighbourhood of habitation!

On the hill behind Letterewe, there is a limestone quarry in the Lewisian gneiss—the oldest Scottish rock formation. It includes rocks that once were laid down as sediments in the sea, and other rocks of igneous origin. Much of it may be a mixture of the two. Here at Letterewe, there are outcrops of rock which are obviously derived from sedimentary rocks. They have, in common with all the Lewisian gneiss, undergone great alterations and re-crystallisations, and the limestone is now in the state of marble. It is, of course, one of the most ancient limestones in the country, formed many ages before the red Torridon sandstones of Slioch, which rises steeply ahead.

The limestone is a white marble, and was worked in a large quarry near the ruined house of Folais. The quarry was linked to the loch by a tramway, and the lime, therefore, would be removed by water.

There is a good story told about Letterewe. When a Mr. Morrison was appointed as Presbyterian minister to the parish of Gairloch, most of the people were still Episcopalians, and they gave the unfortunate Mr. Morrison a very rough time of it. Eventually the poor man managed to get transferred to the parish of Urray.

Mr. Morrison was appointed on 1st March 1711, and it was in September of that year that he happened to go through Letterewe. The Letterewe men pounced upon him, stripped him naked and tied him to a tree, where they left him to the attentions of the Highland midge, which was in full force in the autumn warmth. Eventually, the unfortunate victim was released by a woman who took pity on his sufferings; but the incident gave rise to the saying that since then, there never was a really good and pious man in Letterewe!

But Letterewe is perhaps best known as the site of the

first historic ironworks in Scotland, for it was here in 1607 that Sir George Hay began his smelting operations. The site was on the north bank of the Amhainn na Fuirneis (Stream of the Furnace) on the shore of Loch Maree, a little way to the south-east of Letterewe lodge. But one ought to begin the story at Fasagh near the head of Loch Maree, for Sir George's works are well on in the history of Highland ironworks.

There is no written record of Fasagh, but its methods were a far cry from the first prehistoric bloomeries set up on a windy hill-side, for the wind was the blast in the first iron furnaces.

Fasagh is not the only site of an old ironworks in the Loch Maree area. There are many others whose positions are marked by piles of dark, heavy slag, still rich in iron. But Fasagh is one of the most perfectly preserved sites that we have.

When you have come the long trail from Letterewe southward on the old track; you will, as you come down over the shoulder of Meall Riabhach, see a green flat below you at the mouth of the Abhainn na Fhasaigh. (*Fasagh*, by the way, means a stance, a station; *abhainn* is the Gaelic spelling of our English Avon—meaning water, a stream.) Across the burn, on this green flat, near the loch shore is a lone rowan tree. It is growing upon the site of the old workings.

It is needful to look carefully to see the details of the remains, for the heather is thick over them. But the hollows, three of them, for the furnace beds are to be seen, and three casting hearths. In two of the hearths, ancient tree roots are preserved, set in the dark, heavy slag. Round about, the slag is heaped up in a high bank. Water power from the burn was utilised to operate various pieces of machinery, and remains of sluices are found at the head of the burn where it flows out of Lochan Fada. The workers therefore had some control over their power supply.

The slag is very dark and heavy and still retains over 60 per cent of iron, showing that the smelting methods were not highly efficient. The ore was the brown bog ore that is dug out of the iron pans in the local peat bogs. It is probable that Fasagh was the last works to smelt bog ore direct with charcoal.

Did they get the ore close by? Perhaps a little; most, I think, from the Gairloch area. A number of small pans of bog ore, of good quality, are known on either side of Gairloch bay. At South Erradale, a dry stone wall was once built (in 1845) of the bog ore, and suitably named the Garadh Iaruinn (the iron wall).

Remains found include the tuyere, a heavy casting of iron and now in the Museum of the Scottish Antiquarian Society; a cast metal ring, which formed part of the forge hammer, and the hammer head itself. This last was taken to Kinlochewe and used to make an anvil for the smithy there.

Tradition has it that the workers were English. Tradition points out the Cladh nan Sasunnach (the Englishmen's burying ground) and also the Lochan Cul na Cathrach ("the tarn at the back of the fairies' seat") into which they are said to have thrown their tools on leaving the district. It is a quite probable tradition, for English ironmasters did come north, when Elizabethan and other Acts stopped their using English woods, so that the timber might be kept for the Navy.

Across Loch Maree, the pines of the Coille na Glas-leitire ("the wood of the grey slope"), are a last remnant of the forests that attracted the iron workers to Loch Maree. It was not for iron ore that they came here, for that could be easily imported, but for the woods that meant a good supply of charcoal for smelting. There is no evidence of coal being used for smelting in Scotland until the Carron works began using it, soon after their foundation in 1760. On the other hand, in England, one Simon Sturtevant took out a patent for its use in 1611.

Some idea of the Caledonian Forest around Loch Maree is

given in Sir Donald Monro's *Description of the Western Isles of Scotland*, based on his travels through them in 1549. Of the Island Ewe in Poolewe Bay, he says that it is "full of woods, guid for thieves to wait upon uther mens gaire".

And now, Sir George Hay. He was one of the "Fife Adventurers" who tried to settle in Lewis, or as it was always called, The Lews. The Lewis men had been giving trouble, and it was decided to try and plant a colony there, to foster more peaceful habits. Several attempts were made and failed. At last, Sir George, and two other adventurers, Lord Balmerino and Sir James Spens, sold their rights in the project to MacKenzie of Kintail (who desired The Lews himself and had quietly helped to prevent the settlement), taking in part payment the Letterewe woods for the purpose of iron smelting. This agreement was concluded in 1610; but as a Reverend Farquhar MacRae was appointed minister of Gairloch in 1608 "that he might serve the colony of English which Sir George Hay kept at Letterewe", actual working must have begun at least as early as 1607.

Sir George would, of course, have gone to Poolewe along the old right-of-way to embark for Lewis. He may have passed Fasagh while it was still in operation; he certainly would realise the possibilities of the great woods. It is likely he already knew something about iron working, for, in 1598, he was granted by James VI the Carthusian Priory of Perth and the lands of Errol, which we know to have been an early site of ironworking.

There is little to see of the furnace site at Letterewe, bar some slag turned up in mole hills and in the dyke along the stream side. It is a much lighter slag and paler in colour than that of Fasagh. It only contains from 20-30 per cent of iron, so that methods of working were now much improved. The ore was not only local bog ore, but also imported clayband and haematite. The clayband ironstone may have come from the Scottish Midland Valley; the haematite is identical with that of Lancashire and Cumberland. It would be brought by sea to Poolewe, where it had to be unloaded and taken overland until the navigable part of the River Ewe is reached. There it would be reshipped and sailed down to Letterewe. Sir George also started another works at Talladale, on the opposite side of Loch Maree, and this would get its ore in the same fashion.

It is said that Sir George at one time planned to cut a canal, so as to avoid the tedious unloading and reloading. Two pits, near the south-west corner of Loch Ewe (Poolewe Bay) are said to have been trial holes for this project.

Sir George Hay is said to have cast cannon among other things at Letterewe. Some of the pigs of iron are used by Letterewe to this day, as ballast in their motor boat.

Sir George died Earl of Kinnoull in 1634. The works were apparently carried on for a little time after his death. In 1612, he was granted a virtual monopoly for 31 years to manufacture iron and glass in Scotland, and in 1621, to transport his iron to any port or burgh in Scotland that he wished. Loch Maree must have been the forge of Scotland.

The last works to cease operation, probably about 1668, were those of Red Smiddy (A Cheardach Ruadh), on the banks of the River Ewe where the navigable part of the river ends. The soundings of the Bathymetrical Survey indicate that the "river" above this point is really a long narrow arm of the loch, so that the old ironmasters placed their dam at the end of Loch Maree, where the true river flows out of it and descends to the sea at Poolewe in a series of waterfalls. Later on, cruives for the capture of salmon were set up there. These were removed in 1847, when the Government drainage inspector refused to sanction drainage in Kinlochewe until they were taken away.

The Red Smiddy works lie on the bank of the river on the

c

north-east side, and the remains are fairly extensive. The ore used was haematite and clayband. There is some evidence that the clayband was roasted before it was smelted. The furnace chimney was said to have stood ten feet high in 1852. It was built of the local Torridon sandstone, which has been partially vitrified by the intense heat.

It may be interesting to note that the surnames of Cross, Kemp and Bethune were brought into the Gairloch district by the English ironworkers. One, according to the story, of the three sons of one Cross, one of the last of ironworkers, was a bard. He lived at Kernsary at Innis a'bhaird (the Bard's field) and was known as the Bard Sasunnach. Another of the brothers Cross, Hector, was at the shielings on the slopes of Beinn Lair above Letterewe, when a yellow-haired Highlander came to the door and asked for milk. When he had drunk, he returned the wooden bowl with a gold piece at the bottom.

This was in 1746, and the Gille Buidhe, as he was called, from the yellow colour of his hair, was carrying gold to the fugitive Prince. Of course, the tale of a man with gold about him spread quickly through the district. Early next morning there was a shot heard on the hill, and one of the Letterewe crofters returned quietly to his home to live comfortably on the spoil. Part of the Gille Buidhe's plaid was still in existence in the nineteenth century, when it formed the lining of a coat worn by an old man at Letterewe. This story is the last we hear concerning the Loch Maree ironworkers.

After leaving Letterewe and the houses at Furnace, the way goes on along the flank of Slioch and well above the majority of the birch woods which fringe Loch Maree. One is too close to Slioch to see how the mountain does, in fact, resemble a spear in shape; for the name Slioch means a spear. From the other side of Loch Maree, too, it is easy to see how the isolated height of Torridon sandstone (summit 3,217 ft.) rises from the highly irregular surface of the Lewisian gneiss. On the old track, however, you will walk upon the Lewisian gneiss and sometimes stray on to the Torridonian, and be able to see at close quarters the exact nature of the junction between the two.

In this district the Lewisian must have once formed hilly country. The Torridon sandstone—the debris weathered off this ancient land—is seen enveloping three hills of Lewisian gneiss. One is over 2,000 feet in height. The old valleys between the hills can also be traced.

The Torridon sandstone is supposed to have been deposited either in a cold or an arid climate, because the feldspars, minerals which weather rapidly under ordinary climatic conditions, are quite fresh in the grits and sandstones. Where the Torridonian is seen resting on the gneiss, there are "fossil" screes of fragments of Lewisian gneiss, which were probably weathered-off almost in the place where they now rest.

The road is fairly well made for the next few miles. It is built up, to form a little terrace along the hillside. The burns from Slioch, however, come down in deep, narrow gorges, and here and there the track descends into the rocky hollow and out again, fording the stream, with great sharpness. Without bridges, no cart could go that way.

Along the way, mostly below the level of the road, are the marks of deserted fields, ancient peat cuttings, the ruins of field dykes and the ruins of houses. Even the wide view across Loch Maree to the great Torridon sandstone hills, in Kinlochewe Forest, cannot take the edge off the essential melancholy of this part of the road. The last people left this place some forty or fifty years ago; here one house still retains its chimney stack; here are some holly trees amongst the ruins. Here is the ruin of the life that once was lived upon the shores of Loch Maree.

There are three principal villages represented by these ruins. Their names, beginning in the north-west and going south-east, Innis Ghlas, Coppachy and Regoilachy. Regoilachy was the first to be abandoned.

Beyond the ruins, the way becomes harder. It is no longer a made track, but a faint trace entering a rocky hollow, littered with great blocks of gneiss and with high, almost overhanging, crags above. This is the Clais na Leac (Hollow of the Flag-stones). It is rough and slow going. One emerges at the end into one of the most delightful sites for a house that could be imagined. Under the steep flank of Slioch, lies a level green, cradled in a basin of rocky knolls. To Loch Mareeside, beyond the basin lip, the hillside again falls steeply. The burn comes down the Slioch slopes in a series of long, white cascades, which fall into deep, clear pools. Then the stream meanders across the smooth green flat, and drops again over the edge of the basin to Loch Maree.

Beside the sparkling cascade is a little house, built in warm red Torridon sandstone. But the house is roofless, and no one but the half-wild goats, who peer at you over the rocks, inhabits the ruin of Smiorsair, which once could be called a hamlet.

The way once more takes to a rough, heather-grown and rocky route, upon the flank of Meall Riabhach; from which it descends steeply to the old wooden bridge upon the Abhainn an Fhasaigh, and Fasagh, at the head of Loch Maree.

CHAPTER III

THE COULIN PASS

THE Abhainn an Fhasaigh is a broad and turbulent stream, leaping in waterfalls from pool to pool. Its valley, deep and steep-sided, rises upon the one hand to the terraced red sandstone of Slioch and upon the other, to the great escarpment of Beinn a'Mhuinidh. The rocks are here involved in the great North-West Highland thrusting movements. The silvery escarpment above the river Fhasaigh, which reaches round to Meallan Ghobhar above the head of Loch Maree, is of Cambrian rocks, over which a mass of the ancient Lewisian gneiss has been thrust by the Kinlochewe line of movement. The Moine thrust itself is found farther to the south-west in the valley of the Abhainn Bruachaig.

The road to the south runs under the great crag, where the stream from a mountain loch on Beinn a'Mhuinidh falls in a thin ribbon, its little gorge edged by dark Scots pine and pale green birches, whose spring foliage hangs cobweb-like upon the branches. Kinlochewe is still two miles ahead, but Loch Maree's head is here, below the waterfall.

Kinlochewe—the head of Loch Ewe. The name is witness to the old extent of the loch farther up the glen. It is over the silted-up loch bed that the old track goes, between the alders to the gorse hedges at Culaneilan. Ahead is a great view of Beinn Eighe (The Mountain of the File) whose serrated edge of Cambrian quartzite gives point to its name, and the grey

heights of the Coulin Forest farther away, up the glen toward
Torridon.

Kinlochewe recalls the old name of Loch Maree—Loch Ewe.
Once there were two Loch Ewes, the inland fresh-water one,
and Poolewe Bay. Poolewe Bay is still Loch Ewe. Letterewe
is the hill slope above the Ewe.

From Kinlochewe, the old route to the Coulin Pass climbs
gently up the boggy slopes of the Feith an Leothaid and Carn
Dhomhnuill Mhic a'Ghobha to a height of nearly a thousand
feet, dropping more steeply down to the house at Torran-
cuilinn at the foot of the pass. The present road keeps to the
low ground along the floor of the valley which links Torridon
with Kinlochewe, a private motor road branching up the
Coulin Pass at Loch Clair. The old track is hard to find after
the first short stretch from the chapel on the east bank of the
river from Loch Clair, and the going is fairly tiring. But the
trouble is worth-while, for at 1,000 feet one has a little parity
with Beinn Eighe. From that level, it is possible to grasp the
form of the great mountain with its crest of pinkish Cambrian
quartzites, which spill great screes down his steep slopes like
the mane of a hill pony.

Beinn Eighe's quartzite summit has been the butt of various
jests, to the general effect that he requires no snow to whiten
himself with and that the summer sun never diminishes his
Alpine looking crest. But the Cambrian quartzites are not
the white of snow at all, nor are they white. They may sometimes hold a pinkish flush, more often they are rather pepper
and salt looking; the real snow lingering on the ridge makes
them look extremely grubby.

The hillside up which the track goes, rises steeply above
Loch Clair, then flattens out to rise again in the small crest
that is Carn Dhomhnuill Mhic a'Ghobha (the carn of Donald,
son of the smith). It is to the foot of the ridge that one must
steer one's steps, for that way goes the right-of-way. In dry

weather, the crossing of the flat ground can be made at any point, but it is a bog, and the real line of the road keeps off it, on harder ground, on a slightly higher level.

Climbing up, the way goes across a stream that takes origin from three rocky clefts on the hill above; clefts that are filled with Scots pine and birches. Native Scots pine still survive on the banks of the main stream below. Many of these pines were cut to provide timber for Coulin Lodge. Their annual rings averaged about 250 years, according to a count made on some of the trees then felled. Often the trunks had auger holes in them, from which the Loch Carron people collected the resin for use on their boats.

As I ascended the route, on a misty day, the cloud gradually cleared completely from Beinn Eighe, but still lay in the hollow of Loch Maree. It slowly cleared, breaking up into little fleecy wisps which dappled all the slopes of Slioch. When I reached the top of the ridge, disturbing a herd of fifty red deer, I looked down Glen Torridon toward Loch Torridon, vastly deep, blue and mysterious in the haze. Great columns of mist rose like smoke up the flanks of Liathach, a mountain which leaps sheer and rocky from Torridon glen.

Then too, from the top of the ridge, I could look down and across to Coulin and the Coulin Forest. The name is said to mean the Old Grey Heads. The Cambrian quartzite does, in fact, give this effect, for the hills are rather rounded in outline and grey. In these hills, the rocks are again involved in the north-west Highland thrust movements; on Beinn Liath Mhor (the large grey mountain), for example, a whole hillside forms a kind of real live geological diagram, showing the overfolding and thrusting of Cambrian and Torridonian rocks.

The Coulin Pass itself, leading from the head of Glen Torridon through to Strath Carron, lies far below, a broad, heather-covered valley, with the white road snaking up it, and the hills beyond Strath Carron peeping through the wide gap at its head.

Above Kinlochewe, the ridge which the old track leads on to, is called the Feith an Leothaid—the bog of Leod. There is a rather long and involved story attached to it.

Somewhere about 1350, Kinlochewe was raided by a party of the Earl of Ross's people. Kenneth MacKenzie, the third Lord of Kintail, very naturally gave chase—it was his property —he regained the spoil and killed many of the raiders. The Earl of Ross, however, took immediate revenge. He had MacKenzie executed in Inverness, and seized the lands of Kinlochewe, which he gave to Leod Mac Gilleandreis.

Kenneth MacKenzie, however, had a son, Murdo. He skulked about the Torridon hills, whence he came to be known as Black Murdo of the Caves, hoping for a chance of taking Leod's life. Eventually, the mainland became too hot for him and he retired to Lewis, where lived his uncle MacLeod. Some years later he came back, at the head of a party of men. He happened to meet his old nurse who identified him to her own satisfaction by a black spot on his back, and who gave him information about Leod's movements. The story ends with Murdo's party setting upon Leod and his men at the Feith an Leothaid, and killing them all. Murdo's party cut off the heads of their victims and tossed them into the Kinlochewe river. The heads, instead of floating into Loch Maree, banked up at the ford on the river below Kinlochewe, which has ever since been called Ath-nan-Ceann—the ford of the heads. The name is now corrupted into Athnagown, Anagown and Anancaun (inch-to-the-mile Ordnance map).

Coming down to Torran-cuilinn and tree-fringed Loch Coulin, I lost the line of the old road. However, looking back from the Coulin Pass, the way is quite distinct, white ruts running steeply down through the dark heather.

The way ahead is a long, steady climb. Behind Beinn Eighe rises at the mouth of the glen; ahead are the smooth slopes of the hills about the pass. Native pines grow finely at the Easan

Dorcha bridge, beside the stream, and there is a glimpse of the Beinn Liaths. Higher up the pines die out and the road is edged by peat bog and haggy ground. Slioch comes into view over the shoulder of Carn Dhomhnuill.

Finally, the summit gap, and the view across the deep glen of Strath Carron, to the great mountains beyond, and then the long, gradual descent to Achnashellach through the trees of the Forestry plantations. Under the larch plantations, the grass was a very vivid green, and in it grew big clumps of primroses. Through the trees was a glimpse of Loch Carron, and the little Dughaill which lies in the flat ground at the head of the sea loch. Carron is a sea loch, a fiord, so shut in by the hills that the tangle on its beaches seems completely out of place, and the salt taste of the water incredible. The formation of the deep, steep-sided, lengthy Strath Carron is to be correlated with the presence of a great fault or line of breakage in the rocks along the line of the glen. It is also part of one of the ancient through valleys from the west to the east.

The original route did not make the easy descent to Achnashellach that the present private road does; but dropped steeply from the head of the pass, down the hillside, to Craig, higher up Strath Carron. At Craig, there used to be an inn.

CHAPTER IV

THE THREE GLENS

THE southward way from Poolewe goes through nearly the full range and variety of Highland scenery. It touches upon the three glens that have been held to be Scotland's most beautiful—Strathfarrar, Cannich and Affric. It is a way of argument, for the prowler-about-Scotland is very likely to dispute Affric's claim to be the first glen in the Highlands. Beautiful she may be, but—and it is in the but that lies the road to endless controversy.

The three glens have another significance. Each of them provide ways through the hills from west to east; and the folk in the old days using the Poolewe-Fort Augustus road could join or leave it for their various destinations by any of these glens.

This is the route of the drove road from Craig in Strath Carron to Tomich at the head of Strath Glass. The present road through the Coulin Pass comes down to the Strath at Achnashellach, so the road up Strath Carron has to be followed back to Craig to get on the right-of-way again. From Craig, the way goes up the valley of the Allt a'Chonais. It coincides with the line of a track made to Glenuaig Lodge. From the end of this track, a right-of-way continues, over the watershed into Strath Conon and the Contin district; but the route south diverges before the lodge is reached. It turns up the valley of the Crom-allt (bent stream, from a sharp angle in its course), and climbs over the hills between Bidean an Eoin Deirg and Carn nam Fiaclan, to the headwaters of the Amhainn Srath Mhuilich. It follows this stream down to little Loch Mhuilich, and goes on down the valley to Loch Monar at the head of Glen Strath-farrar.

The way is now open to go to the west by various hill passes. One descends into the valley of the River Ling, and then can reach either Strath Carron or Loch Long (on Loch Duich) by means of a good network of old tracks. The way south, however, turns along Loch Monar side and goes down Glen Strathfarrar to Inchvuilt. Here it crosses the river Farrar and clambers over the bealach between Meallan Odhar and An Soutar, to arrive in the middle part of Glen Cannich.

Again, one can follow through tracks to the west, or go eastward into Strath Glass. The west-going track leads up Glen Cannich and over the main Scottish watershed to Glen Elchaig and the Loch Duich district. The eastward route is that of the present road, by Struy and the Druim Pass to Beauly and Inverness. Muir of Ord is also an important destination, for here used to be held big cattle fairs.

The Fort Augustus route goes down Glen Cannich, crossing the mouth of Glen Affric, and reaches Tomich, from which it goes over the hills to the Great Glen.

It will, therefore, be seen that anyone following out the line of the Poolewe-Fort Augustus track, is given the chance of exploring the Three Glens and considering their rival claims.

What makes the beauty that men seek amongst mountains? Here in the Three Glens there is a little of the Trossachs style, but it is mixed with the wider spaces of the far North, and the higher peaks of the more central mountains. Here are mountains and hillsides where the heather grows. Here are lochs. Here are clear rivers and waterfalls where the water is amber stained with peat. Here are great natural woods of birch and pine. "An eye accustomed to flowery pastures and waving harvests is astonished and repelled by this wide extent of hopeless sterility. The appearance is that of matter incapable of form or usefulness, dismissed by nature from her care and disinherited of her favours, left in its original elemental state, or quickened only with one sullen power of useless vegetation.''

Thus wrote Dr. Johnson of Highland scenery, in his account of his journey to the Western Isles. It is well to remember that it is only within very recent times, that men have come to enjoy mountain scenery. Nor, of course, did Dr. Johnson set foot in the Three Glens. But he justified the visitor to the mountains: ''Regions mountainous and wild, thinly inhabited, and little cultivated, make a great part of the earth, and he that has never seen them, must live unacquainted with much of the face of nature, and with one of the great scenes of human existence.''

The Three Glens are three of the longest glens in Scotland, and they bear a general resemblance to each other. Each has a fine loch at its head: Loch Affric in Glen Affric, Loch Mullardoch in Glen Cannich, and Loch Monar in Glen Strathfarrar. Each has a fine river flowing from the loch at its head and other lochs along the lower part of the valley. Each has high mountains rising upon either hand. Loch Monar is cradled amongst high peaks; between Strathfarrar and Cannich is Sgurr na Lapaich (3,773 ft.); between Cannich and Affric, the mass of Mam Sodhail (3,862 ft.) and Carn Eige (3,877 ft.).

But perhaps the finest feature of the glens are their natural woods, last remnants of the Caledonian Forest. They are of Scots pine and birch. Sometimes the two trees mingle, sometimes they form separate woods. In autumn, the birches are a fire of pure gold, against which the pines stand dark and sombre. In winter, the birches are silver-barked and crimson-twigged against the blue skies and the snow on the heights; whilst the pines are vivid blue-green, ruddy barked. In spring, the pollen is yellow on the pines, and the birches are a delicate veil of green. In the heat of summer, the air is heavy with the scent of the pines; whilst the sunlight filters through the watered silk of the birch leaves, to form a mosaic of light and limpid shadow on the ground.

Very approximately, for there are plenty of exceptions; the birches seem to prefer the southern exposures and the pines, the northern. That is, the pines are mainly upon the south slopes of the glen, and the birches on the north. This segregation has been noticed in all the natural Highland woodlands.

Both birches and pines are large, well-grown trees. I was told that a pine felled in Glen Strathfarrar had 370 annual rings as well as others too close-grained to count. The birches are tall and fairly straight, but are smaller than those employed in building the crannog (lake dwelling) on Loch Treig. In this structure, the birch trunks were straight like pine logs, without pronounced taper; annual rings numbered 118 in one trunk. Loch Treig is, to-day, devoid of any natural forest. Straight, long trunks are, of course, indicative of growth in a fairly dense forest.

The natural woodland of the Highlands has a special beauty in its undergrowth, which is lost in the new, closely planted woods. The trees are far enough apart to allow of tall heather, tapering junipers, blaeberries and other plants forming a thick undergrowth. Amongst them, the big wood ants build great conical nests of pine needles.

The rocks of the Three Glens are principally Moine schists, though in this district, the older Lewisian sometimes appears, where the covering of Moine over it has been stripped off. In Glen Strathfarrar, a Lewisian marble, white and coarsely crystalline, is exposed near Inchvuilt, the point at which the track south crosses the Farrar. Lewisian marble, varying from white to green in colour, is also found east of Strathmore Lodge on Loch Monar, where the track south comes down to the lochside.

Graphite ("black lead") was once worked in Glen Strathfarrar, in the Moine schists, on the north bank of the Farrar, a little below Loch a'Mhuilinn. It was worked for a short time at the beginning of the nineteenth century, but was abandoned when the price of graphite fell. The cost of carting it away was also very high. In 1818, five tons are said to have been produced at a cost of £13 per ton; they were sold for £93 per ton.

About the same time, there was intermittent working of the lead mines which lie between Strath Glass and Glen Strathfarrar. The veins are found on the hill near Loch na Meine (the lake of the mine). The ore is of high grade, but the mining operations were on a small scale and do not seem to have made much profit.

Loch Monar, at the head of Strathfarrar, where the old track comes into the Three Glens, is a strange place. The loch lies in the lap of high hills and all around the grey rocks are intensely smoothed and rounded by the passage over them of ice during the glacial period. I felt caged in by the hills. During the waning period of the Ice Age, Loch Monar seems to have actually caged in its hollow a large volume of ice. It is described as an "ice cauldron". The ice escaped out of the cauldron westward, northward and eastward; but in the later stages it only flowed out to the east—down Glen Strathfarrar. To-day, the actual lip of the rock basin in which Loch Monar lies, is silted up by the waste brought down by the Allt Coire na Faochaige.

Leaving the Monar basin, having passed a jagged bit of schist with S and 15 on it, which I take to indicate the distance to Struy Inn, the road runs for a short distance in the ravine of the Garbh Uisge. Here the water pours in falls over the rocks, at the bottom of a rock-flanged gorge, to whose sides a few pines cling precariously. The name means just this state of affairs—Garbh Uisge, rough water. Rough is perhaps a poor translation of the Gaelic *garbh*: it seems to mean broken country—rocks, waterfalls, crags, sharp peaks. A Gaelic speaker said to me the other day, when we were trying to get a ewe turned out of my ground, which beast was making a determined attempt to get stuck on a ledge above a waterfall, "I'd no idea the burn was so rough". At this point the burn has a high cascade, a pool and an overhanging, tree-hung crag.

The Garbh Uisge unites with the Uisge Misgeach a little farther on, and becomes the River Farrar; the road comes gently down to the level green flats of Broulin. Here the eastward road goes on down the glen to Struy and Strath Glass; the Fort Augustus track turns across the river at Inchvuilt near Broulin lodge, and goes gently up through Inchvuilt wood to cross over to Glen Cannich.

Broulin is a pleasing level spot, on which an army might pitch their camp. Fairly recently, a Charles I shilling was found there; dropped by a soldier of an army who did indeed camp there.

That army was led by General Monck. It will be recalled that after the Battle of Worcester (1651) the Commonwealth soldiers overran Scotland. Various chiefs, however, held out for the Stewart cause, including Lochiel and Glengarry; and it was to deal with these rebels that General Monck came north in 1654, and carried out a rapid march through the Highlands. His force included his own regiment, which is now the Coldstream Guards. Here is part of General Monck's report. They had come from Glengarry to Glen Quoich, and then crossed into Kintail.

The violent storms in the Hills drove about 500 cowes sheepe and goates for shelter into the Glen, which was brought in by the soulders. Wee had notice that Middleton's [the Royalist leader] Horses were gone to Glenelg that night. The 27th [of June] the Army came to Lough-Els [Loch Alsh], where the Enemy had also bin and left 3 barrels of powder with some store of provisions behinde them for haste. In all our march from Glenroy wee burn'd the houses and cottages of the MacMartin's and others in armes and in all parts of Seaforth's Country.

The 29th I came to Glen-teugh [probably lon Fhiodha] in the Shields of Kintale; the night was very tempestuous and blew down most of the tents. In all this march wee saw only 2 women of the inhabitants, and one man. The 30th the army march't from Glen-teugh to Browling [Broulin], the way for neere 5 miles soe boggie that about 100 baggage horses were left behinde, and many other horses begg'd or tir'd. Never any Horse men (much lesse an armie) were observ'd to march that way. The soulders mett with 500 cattell, sheepe, and goates, which made some part of amends for the hard march.

The bog, where the horses were lost, on the way from Glen Elchaig in Kintail over to the head of Loch Monar, is still called the Bog of the Horses, and many remains of the beasts have been dug out of it.

The massif of Mam Sodhail dominates Cannich and Affric glens. It is really a group of heights—each of which have their separate names. Carn Eige, the highest, is the highest mountain north of the Great Glen, and twelfth highest in Scotland. Mam Sodhail, which should be spelled Sabhal, means the Rounded Hill of Barns. It was so called because of the rich grass upon it, and hence the number of barns for cattle that were on it. But it is all a lonely desert now, given up to deer for the most part.

Both Mam Sodhail and Sgurr na Lapaich were important points when the principal triangulation of Great Britain was done by the Ordnance Survey. The surveyors on Sgurr na Lapaich, between 15th July and 25th October 1846, identified Ben More in South Uist (84 miles), Clisham, North Harris (77 miles), Ben Klibreck (64 miles), Corriehabbie (70 miles), Ben Macdhui (56 miles) and Ben Nevis (40 miles) among other peaks. Two years later, they were on Mam Sodhail from 29th July to 31st August and observed Ben More, Mull (68 miles),

GLEN STRATHFARRAR

The pattern of native wood, stream and mountain
which builds the peculiar beauty of the Three
Glens is nowhere better seen than in Glen
Strathfarrar.　An important east-west cross
country track goes through Strathfarrar as well
as the route from Poolewe to Fort Augustus.

Ben More, South Uist (81 miles), The Storr (43 miles), Clisham, North Harris (79 miles), Ben Wyvis (34 miles), Corriehabbie (72 miles), Ben Macdhui (56 miles), Glas Maol (72 miles), Ben Lawers (61 miles) and Ben Nevis (34 miles).

Some of the place names here are interesting. The Uisge Misgeach, which flows into the Farrar, is the Water of Intoxication. Cannich is from the Gaelic *Cannach*—cotton grass— and all along the low-lying, boggy flats in these glens the cotton grass spreads its silky white tufts. Affric means dappled water. Strath Glass, into which the Three Glens open, is from a word glais, a stream: the strath of the stream. Tomich, from which the track south begins to climb over to Glen Moriston, is the place of knolls (*Tom*, a knoll).

Affric and Cannich are busy places now. Beside ruined and empty houses and deserted pastures, new works are pushing ahead. There are mechanical diggers, lorries, jeeps, Nissen huts, steam rollers, men at work. For Affric and Cannich are to have their waters harnessed to provide electric power for the Highlands: power that may provide a means of bringing back the lost population and the lost industry; power that can mean not only beauty in the glens, but life and work.

The Affric hydro-electric scheme has been the subject of much controversy. Many people wanted, and still want, to keep the glen and its neighbourhood "unspoiled", deserted save for sportsmen, mountaineers and a few shepherds. After all, one need not notice the old ruins along the glens.

But to the walker who has come from Poolewe, on the old track southward, past the roofless houses on the side of Slioch, the lorries sinking in the muddy passing bays to let a jeep by, are the symbol of a new hope for the Highlands. Perhaps the Sleeping Beauty is awakening.

D

CHAPTER V

THE OUTLET TO THE SOUTH

FROM Tomich in Strath Glass, the road to Fort Augustus climbs over the ridge to Glen Moriston. It goes by Guisachan and the east bank of the Eas Socach, to the high bare moor, where Loch na Beinne Baine lies like a blue jewel in the dark heather.

At Loch na Beinne Baine (the lake of the milk mountain), it is possible to see the old track, as a broad trace in the moorland, curling up onto the stony ridge beyond the loch. The track keeps east of the loch and then turns slightly westward on to the watershed ridge between Glen Moriston and Strath Glass. There are a number of little cairns on the ridge. Behind, one can still see the snow wreaths in the corries of Mam Sodhail. Ahead, lies the Great Glen and the way to the south.

The right-of-way drops down from the ridge in a rather sinuous course upon the western flanks of Beinn Bhreac (the brindled mountain, from its many rock outcrops) and Meall na Doire (the round hill of the wood) and reaches Glen Moriston near Torgyle Bridge. There used to be an inn at Torgyle. The route crosses the Moriston River (the place name here, Boat of Inverwick, is significant of one way of getting over), and climbs over the ridge between Glen Moriston and Fort Augustus and the Great Glen.

But between Loch na Beinne Baine and Torgyle; that is the problem. These moorland uplands, which rise to 2,000 feet, are undulating, heathery expanses, dotted with rock outcrops.

They have no marked feature to guide the stranger's step. And the track? There is no track to-day.

I found the line of a track by ascending from Torgyle to the loch on the ridge, but I doubt that I could find it down again. It is easier to follow faint trails uphill. You may catch the faint dent in the heather skyline where the ruts still affect the growth; you may catch the shape of a cairn on a ridge. Down-hill, the cairns, if they are small, mingle with the other loose boulders about.

Blessed indeed are they who build cairns. Walking this moor, here and there, quite frequently one finds three rocks piled together, one on the other, the work of man. This way surely then, some trail went, and this way is to be followed. Cairns are the most useful things in the world. Properly placed, where you can catch sight of them against the skyline, they will give you a lead on the right way to follow to reach them. People with time on their hands and a sure knowledge of the track they are following, might do worse than build more cairns to help the erring steps of those who follow after.

To the west, across the moor, one looks to the mighty ridge of Sgurr nan Conbhairean (3,634 ft.). This rocky crest, in whose corries the snow lies long into summer, is part of Drum Alban, the great north-south mountain range of Scotland which parts the eastern waters from the western. The names mean the Peak of the Dog Men or hunters; the end of the ridge to the north is the Tigh mor na Seilge—the Great House of the Hunting. Here, story relates, the Fingalian hunters would begin the day's sport and pursue the chase for twenty miles across country to Ach'nan Conbhairean (the Field of the Hunters) above Invermoriston.

As a matter of history, it was in a cave in one of the corries of this range that Prince Charles met the Seven Men of Glenmoriston (who later became the Eight Men, after Hugh McMillan met them by accident and joined them). These seven men, seeing that they could not live in safety in their homes, whilst the soldiers ravaged the country after Culloden, bound themselves together by a solemn oath and took to the hills, from which they waged a private war on the military. The Prince was with them for some time—almost three weeks.

The Seven Men took an oath, when the Prince joined them, that "their backs should be to God and their faces to the devil, that all the curses the Scriptures did pronounce might come upon themselves and all their posterity if they did not stand firm to the Prince in the greatest dangers, and if they should discover to any person—man, woman, or child—that the Prince was in their keeping, till once his person should be out of danger". None of them, in fact, spoke of Charles having been with them until a year after he had left Scotland. They ventured out to Fort Augustus to get bread for the Prince and brought back a pennyworth of gingerbread as a special luxury for him! They got some better clothing for him by the expedient of shooting some servants carrying baggage for the soldiers' officers.

The Seven Men, Patrick Grant, the three brothers Hugh, Alexander and Donald Chisholm, Alexander MacDonald, John MacDonald (alias Campbell) and Grigor MacGregor, of course conversed in Gaelic, but it was arranged that everything they said should be translated to the Prince. The result of this translation was that he quite stopped their regular use of bad language!

Patrick Grant told Bishop Forbes, who compiled *The Lyon in Mourning* that with living so much out on the hills, the Prince was troubled with lice. He said that the Prince was very nimble on the hills in the daytime but at night he stumbled into bog holes and was "plashed up to the navel, having no breeches, but a philabeg, and when he had arrived at any place to take a little rest, he would have taken a nook of his plaid and therewith have rubbed his belly and thighs to clean them the best way he could" (*Lyon in Mourning*, Vol. III).

But the road to the south only takes a distant view of the cave of the Seven Men. Distantly too, one can look up the glen in which Loch Loyne sparkles; and up to the mountains of Cluanie.

Perhaps the view in front is the most interesting, for in front is the way south. It is a curious view, unusual in that it includes the two hill passes over which the track goes—the lower ridge between Glen Moriston and the Great Glen, and, seen rising above it, the heights of Corrieyairack, over which the road to Dalwhinnie runs. Corrieyairack, built by General Wade, rises to a height of 2,507 feet and until it went out of use as a road, was the highest road in the country. Snow may linger there even in June, and be right across the track in May.

So, the end of the road from Poolewe to Fort Augustus is in sight. There is the faint trail up from Glen Moriston through the woods to the ridge above Fort Augustus, and just below the top of the ridge, the way joins the military road from Fort Augustus to Glenelg. Then it is over the top and down to the great hollow of the Great Glen, which runs across Scotland, north-east, south-west, cradling the lochs of Linnhe, Lochy, Oich and Ness. The hollow is excavated along the line of an ancient fault which crosses the Highlands like a knife cut. Movement still goes on along the line of fracture, and there are sometimes minor earthquakes in the district. Above the glen, rises Ben Nevis, easily in sight on a clear day from the old track.

And from Fort Augustus, where? South by the direct route over Corrieyairack where the military road is still easily followed? North-eastward up the Great Glen to Inverness? South-westward down the Glen to Lochaber? All these ways are open and were open to the folk who came from the north-western Highlands. The main flow of traffic would be southward. That way would go the droves to the south country markets. Falkirk at one time, was a great centre and had a large cattle fair. In Gaelic, Falkirk was known as An Eaglais Bhreac—the brindled church!

Sheep were taken over the old road, from Strathcarron to Fort Augustus in the 1890's. In the first World War, some cattle were taken on the same track from Patt on Loch Monar to Achnashellach. But it is well out of use now.

The old track, of course, might be the basis of a very useful modern cross-country route. So might Corrieyairack. Corrieyairack, admittedly, is always snowed up in winter, but it is not always winter. It avoids the long, "two sides of a triangle" route of the present road system for anyone trying to go from Fort Augustus to Dalwhinnie. To do this to-day by road, one has to go either to Inverness and then turn back on one's tracks (or do much the same, via Strath Errick) or go to Spean Bridge and up past Loch Laggan.

The old track from Fort Augustus over to Glen Moriston also cuts off a long way round. Now, one must go seven miles to Invermoriston and go up the glen from there, instead of arriving in the middle of the glen, after only five miles of travel.

If the Highlands are ever to support a reasonably sized population and industry, some of these angular corners of modern road will have to be cut off.

III

THE ROAD OF THE DEAD

CHAPTER VI

GLEN GARRY TO GLEN MORISTON

AMONG the strange and half-magical cures for human ills that lingered late in the Highlands—in fact, still linger— there runs a peculiar belief in the special power of water or of a stone taken from a place over which both the living and the dead pass. That such a place—the shadowy ground below the road bridge—can be found on every route, is linked with the Highland habit of carrying their dead long distances to burial in some specially hallowed ground.

Coffins went over most Highland roads on men's shoulders, but some of the ways are specially linked with the dead, and of these, the "coffin road" from Seanna-bhaile in Glen Garry to the ancient graveyard at Achlain in Glen Moriston is one.

Glen Garry, striking off from the Great Glen at Loch Oich, is a pleasant valley. It is clothed in trees on its lower slopes, birch and beech, thickets of rhododendron, Scots pine, the trim plantations of the Forestry Commission. Here and there is a gnarled and rotten stump of some great oak of the "faire oakenwood" that once grew upon the north side of the glen. On a quiet summer day, the trees are reflected in the still waters of Loch Garry, and above the woods rise the bare slopes of the hills leading ever higher to the cone of Ben Tee and the mighty ridge of the Sron a'Choire Garbh. Here one would think a man might rest content, without longing to leave Glen Garry for the green meadows of Glen Moriston. It is a steep way to carry a heavy coffin, over the 2,000 foot heights of Ceann a'Mhaim (the Breast Rock), and down the rough slopes to Achlain. And indeed, the original MacDonells of Glen Garry would hardly have welcomed such an idea. But the people who were native to Glen Garry, were turned out to make way for the sheep.

The sheep evictions there, took place in 1772. The Glen Garry estate was managed by the mother of the chief, who was not then of age, and it was she who determined to remove every crofter in the glen. Notices to quit were served, and the tenants told they would be shipped to Australia. Shipping space not being available, this destination was later changed to North America. Those who refused to move had their houses burned over their heads, so as to leave them without any shelter.

Glen Garry is still very largely the same desert that was left after 1772; but slowly, men began to filter back into the glen. Most of them came from Glen Moriston, and when they died, it was natural that they should wish to lie with their ancestors in Achlain graveyard.

The sheep is a devouring monster. It has not only cleared the Highland glens of men; sent back good land to sour and grown brackens and rushes; but has done other, less obvious deeds of evil. It has eaten the young trees, so that the natural forest cannot regenerate itself. It has eaten the best of the wild flowers. No one now can probably tell how much of the old Scottish flora has been so devoured and stamped out. Especially in spring, when the hill grass is late in growing, are sheep dangerous to flowers. Dangerous is not to put it too seriously. Why, for instance, has Scotland no early primroses? Because the sheep regard them as a tasty morsel. Scotland before the coming of the great sheep walks must have been a very different land to look upon.

I picked up the line of the coffin road by the grocer's shop in Glen Garry, at the bridge over the Aldernaig Burn, and began to follow it through a wood of spruce, Scots pine and birch. The delicate greens of the leafing birch and beech contrasted with the dark blue-green of the pines; below the trees, tumbled boulders were covered by thick moss, starry with wood sorrel. The Aldernaig Burn cascaded over rocks beside the pathway.

When there was the great oak wood on the north side of Glen Garry, and a great pine wood upon the south, of which the present trees are only scraps, iron was smelted here. There are remains of small bloomeries all along Loch Garry side; and in 1730, an English company started smelting works on the riverside at Invergarry. Some of their pigs are forming headstones at Gairlochy graveyard farther down the Great Glen. The manager was one Thomas Rawlinson, and story goes that he evolved the modern form of the kilt—the *feile beag* or little kilt, in distinction to the belted kilt or *breacan an fheilidh* (plaid of the kilt). It is said that the folds of the belted kilt, which is merely a large plaid which is wrapped about the middle and secured with a belt—the end being thrown over the shoulder—got in the way of the workers' arms, and Rawlinson suggested that they should discard the upper part of the garment. But the same tale goes for truth with regard to one Parkinson in another part of the country; and the *feile beag* (English, philabeg) is probably just as ancient as the belted kilt. Which garment was worn would depend on the presence of an expert tailor in the district.

The Glen Garry ironworks had a very short life, for the fuel was soon exhausted. It is said that they made 2,450 tons of pig-iron, but that it was of inferior quality and fetched only £5 10s. a ton, compared with £8 per ton paid for the pig-iron of the Furness Company in England.

The path through the wood soon joins the wide track from Faichem. It is very pleasant walking there, with the cone of Ben Tee, still striped with spring snows, peeping through the birch boughs. Men say that the stones for Invergarry Castle on the Raven's Rock (Creag an Fhithich) above Loch Oich, were brought in a human chain from the very summit.

The wood ends at a deer fence, and the track comes out on to open moorland, a pattern of undulating heathland with grey boulders and crags and a few gnarled birches. Ahead, are the brown hills which divide Glen Moriston from Glen Garry.

I came quickly to Loch Lundie, the road dipping down to boat-houses and stables, amongst a plantation of firs and groups of rhododendrons. Behind, Ben Tee and the arc of the Sron a'Choire Garbh were fully in view, springing high above the moorland plateau that fringes the rift of the Great Glen. Then, as I rounded the farther end of Loch Lundie, Ben Nevis appeared through the lifting cloud, with gleaming snow on the dark rock.

Loch Lundie is a silver mirror scattered with islands, set in the dull brown of the moors. From the islands, seagulls rose in screaming clouds. One island, at least, is artificial, a little round mound of stones with a cairn of flagstones and a clumpy green bush upon it. Two of the other islands, formed of natural crops of schist and larger and more irregular in shape than the crannog, I saw were joined with the shore by stepping-stones.

Allan MacRanald's name is linked with that of Loch Lundie: a man I cannot help but admire if it be true that he leaped the Allt a'Ghiubhais and ran down the slopes of Ruskich Wood. He is a man of two fames: the devil incarnate to his enemies, and the gallant, resourceful hero to his friends.

There was feud between the Glen Garry MacDonells and the Ross-shire MacKenzies. The MacKenzies took Strome Castle from the MacDonells and the MacDonells planned revenge. Young Allan disguised himself as a pedlar and penetrated MacKenzie country; returning home to Glen Garry to lead a raiding party, in September 1603, to Kilchrist.

There, story goes, the MacDonells caught the people in the church on Sunday morning and burned them there, forcing those who tried to escape back into the flames. The MacDonell piper strutted round the building composing a pibroch, which tune, Kilchrist, became a great favourite with the MacDonells.

That there was a raid on Kilchrist is historic fact, but there is no evidence of the roasting of the MacKenzies in the kirk, and many people believe that there has been confusion in a memory of an earlier MacDonald raid, in 1487, when the church at Contin, full of MacKenzies seeking sanctuary, was fired.

The traditional story goes on to tell how the MacDonells made their way back to Glen Garry via the level flat below the mountain of Mealfuarvonie above Loch Ness. There, they encamped for the night. Meantime the MacKenzies were up in arms and after them. Suddenly, they attacked over the shoulder of Mealfuarvonie. The MacDonells were completely routed, and ever since the ground has been called Lón na Fola—the Meadow of Blood

Allan ran for his life. Across the peat moss and out on to the sheer crags that rise above Loch Ness and to which cling the trees of Ruskich Wood. A party of MacKenzies ran hot on his heels. There seemed to be no escape. Suddenly, Allan sprang from the crag across the gorge of the burn called the Allt a'Ghiubhais (burn of the pines), which spills down the heights of Ruskich Wood in a great series of cascades. Leum a'Chennaiche, the map marks it, the Merchant's Leap, in memory of Allan's disguise as a spy; Leum Ailein Mhic Ranald, they call it in Glen Moriston, Allan MacRanald's leap.

One of the MacKenzies sprang after him, missed his footing, saved himself by clinging to a sapling. Allan turned and sliced the young branch through, exclaiming as the MacKenzie dropped to his death on the rocks below, "I have left much with your clan this day; let me leave them that also". Meanwhile, the other MacKenzies dashed back to a ford a little way farther up the burn and the chase continued down the rocks of Ruskich Wood to Loch Ness, into which Allan plunged.

Opposite, Fraser of Foyers had seen something going on, and now put out in his boat and fished Allan out. Allan made good his escape, but the hunt went on, and he lived a fugitive life for some time after.

For a time, Allan had a "hide" on one of the Loch Lundie islands. One day, the MacKenzies found this out, and surrounded the loch when darkness fell. Allan was quite alone, but with great presence of mind, suddenly dashed out, shouting, as if to a strong force. "Our common enemy is here. Surround them!" The MacKenzies took to their heels and fled. Allan, who was a skilful archer, rushed after them, and managed to pick off 21 men as they passed over the skyline against the faint light of the sky.

Allan removed from the Loch Lundie islands to a cave on the hillside, which he got a south country mason to make for him. Frightened that the mason might betray him, he paid him, then as the man turned away, struck him down. In his old age Allan is said to have remarked that he hoped for forgiveness for Kilchrist but not for the murder of the faithful mason.

From Loch Lundie, a little east of the mouth of the Allt Lundie, a faint trace of a track goes off up the hillside, becoming plainer as it climbs. It passes a sheep-fank and crosses the Allt Lundie on a wooden bridge by some waterfalls. It then goes on up the slope, to come out on a height above the Milk Loch—Loch a'Bhainne.

Now this track is no mere mark on the hillside, but has some attempt at a surface, and there are flags laid across the drains. Yet above Loch a'Bhainne, it dies a sudden death in a peat hag where the ground levels out, and thereafter is seen no more.

Loch a'Bhainne is a wide spread of water, a little smaller than Lundie, and with green turf at its head. It lies cradled in rocky, brown hills—Meall a'Chrom Dhoire, Meall nam Fairneag and Meall nam Calman. The Allt Bhainne flowing from it falls steeply down to Glen Garry The glen itself is out of view, but Ben Tee rises beyond the loch.

Looking back, Loch Lundie lay still and smooth; with two little glittering tarns in a fold of the brown moor beyond it. The Great Glen seemed hardly a glen; rather a mere fold in the hills among many folds in the hills. Corrieyairack, with snow wreaths still across its track, and the hills of Laggan, heavy with snow; the massive tableland of Glen Doe; the jagged edge of Beinn a'Bhacaidh above Fort Augustus; the long high line of the Lochaber Hills. The skylarks sang constantly, but the country was brown and dead, the heather burnt as by fire in the fierce winter frosts of 1947.

Three burns run into the Loch a'Bhainne and any one of them takes you to the watershed ridge above Glen Moriston. The ridge rises gently, to end in the rocky mound of Mam a'Chroisg (2,303 ft.) and the sharper mass of Meall Dubh (2,581 ft.). Ceann a'Mhaim (2,203 ft.) over which the coffin road passes, is out of sight.

One assumes the coffin road took the driest and easiest line to Ceann, but I found no definite track, and after tiring of the peat hags, found fair going along the side of the Allt Lundie, which comes cascading down from Ceann. It is a lovely burn. The Moine schists here are flaggy grey rocks, lying horizontal or rolling over in great folds over which the water slides in green-white ripples down into cool rocky pools, amber with peat stain. There was frog spawn in one of the pools as I went up by the burnside; in the hot sun it was pleasant to stop and dabble in the water, too pleasant in fact, for I began to feel that all the world, past, present and future, lay beside the rippling burn, and that I had no reason either to go on or to go back.

Higher still, the Allt Lundie turns sharply into the heart of Ceann a'Mhaim, and there is a little group of tarns at its turning. A herd of red deer were searching for food by these pools and I came suddenly on them over the hill. They turned, one by one, pricking up their ears and looking, and then bunched together and trotted off up the flank of Ceann, their coats light brown against the dead heather.

Coming off Ceann a'Mhaim, the line of the coffin road shows as a faint path, soon to be lost again. There, where the hags about the watershed meet the rocky crops of Ceann a' Mhaim, on a little flat overlooking Glen Moriston are the cairns.

When a coffin was carried over a Highland track, there were regular resting places at which the coffin would be set down and food and drink taken by the bearers. Here, on the watershed ridge between Glen Moriston and Glen Garry is such a halting place. The little group of cairns, some large, some small, some half-hidden in the heather, record the stop of each party, for everywhere the coffin was rested a cairn was built to the memory of the dead. Each cairn represents a Glen Moriston man coming back for the last time to Achlain. *Sìth do d'anam, is clach air do chàrn*, runs the saying—Peace to your soul, and a stone on your cairn.

Every friend of the dead man, who could not attend the funeral, would add a stone to the cairn when next he passed that way. *Am fear nach meudaich an carn, g'a meudaich e chroich* —who will not increase the cairn, may he augment the gallows. But that saying may have a double meaning, for cairns are also very valuable landmarks.

It is a tremendous spot, this group of cairns on Ceann a'Mhaim. On the one hand rise the rocks, where snow lingers yet in the sun; on the other the brown peat hag of Druim a'Chathair. Out of the peat bog sprang the round craggy hillock of Carn Mhic Raonuill, which Fort Augustus people call Carn

Funeral Cairns on Ceann A' Mhaim on the Coffin Road from
Glen Garry to Glen Moriston

The Bridge and sheep Fank on the site of Aonach Inn,
Glen Moriston

Allan. Either way, it means the same thing, the Carn of Allan of Lundie.

Across the ridge, the hills beyond the Great Glen—Corrie-yairack, Glen Doe, Beinn a'Bhacaidh, are still in sight. In front, the ground drops steeply to the green meadows of Glen Moriston through which the Moriston river snakes. Far below is a white house, with a grey slate roof, this side of the river from Achlain graveyard.

Beyond the fields, the brown hills rise again, to Sgurr nan Conbhairean; and the eye ranges up the valley toward Cluanie Forest, or over the line of the old track to Poolewe, and the hills of Glen Affric, snow-flecked.

Across the moor, too faint to be picked out at a distance, east of the coffin road, runs the line of the military road from Fort Augustus to Glenelg, which also came down to Achlain. Mealfuarvonie rises like a round lump from the moor farther away, from Lón na Fola, across which Allan MacRanald ran for his life.

The way down is steep and rough, through heather, and the trace of the path is again lost. In the glen, the river has to be forded, before one reaches the road's end—the little burial ground of Achlain.

E

IV

THE CATTLE ROAD FROM THE ISLES

CHAPTER VII

THE CASTLES OF TEILBA

WHEN black cattle were one of the chief exports of the Highlands, great herds came to the mainland from the Isles, to be driven over the drove roads to the southern markets. They might change hands several times on the way. In Kintail, for instance, the cattle were bought by drovers from Perthshire and Ayrshire, who took them farther south to retail them to drovers from England.

It must have been a long journey, for the cattle could not go a very long march each day. They had to eat as they went, and usually were much improved in condition at the end of the trip. Sheep, in the later days of droving, would only do about eight or ten miles a day. The black cattle might do rather more. At night, they were penned in "stances", which were built at intervals along the routes and for the use of which the owner charged so much per head of cattle.

The cattle from Skye, and also from the Long Island (the Outer Hebrides), came across the narrow straits of Kyle Rhea to Glenelg, and went southward over the Bealach Aoidhdailean to Kinloch Hourn, then by Glen Garry to Lochaber. Others probably went over Mam Ratagain and through Glen Shiel and Glen Moriston to Corrieyairack. Mam Ratagain became a military road; the Bealach Aoidhdailean is still a track. It is the drove road over this bealach and to Glen Garry that we are now to follow.

The tides run fierce in the narrow Kyle Rhea. Skye is a stone's throw over the blue, dancing water; there is a jetty for the ferry and grey rocks with tufts of pink stonecrop. Across this little channel, the black cattle used to be made to swim. In spite of the tides, very few were lost. The old *Statistical Account* (1795) tells us that about 2,000 used to cross each year.

Round the headland, on the edge of the shore, are the stone-built remains of an old market stance in which cattle could be folded after being sold. But the view ahead is perhaps more likely to hold one's attention. Glenelg Bay lies placid in the bright sun, the blue sea edged by yellow shingle beaches, the smell of tangle on the warm air, the green flats beyond the sea, the green hills and their rocky crags rising all about the bay. The village of Glenelg is intensely green. Here one is again on Lewisian rocks and Lewisian marble is prominent among them. Where limestone occurs, there is always a special greenness in the vegetation; this must be the secret of Glenelg.

Here are lush meadows, where the meadow sweet and cat's ear valerian mingles with ragged robin and yellow iris; green hillsides which are spangled with primroses and violets in the spring, and now in summer, guarded by the sentinel armies of purple foxgloves. Here cottages can boast of a hedge of honeysuckle. And whatever way you would go from the village, you must climb over high and rocky hills.

Between Kyle Rhea and Glenelg lie the few houses of Galltair. On the flat at the head of the bay are the ruins of the barracks of Bernera which stood at the end of the military road from Fort Augustus. An older fort stood on the high crags above Galltair.

This ancient building, which was of drystone and earth, is Caisteal MhicLeod—MacLeod's Castle. Most of it has been removed, because the Galltair people got their stones there for their houses. Transport was no difficulty—they pushed

Glen Elg Bay and the old Market Stance

The Broch of Dun Grugaig and Gleann Beag, Glen Elg

them over the edge of the crag and built their houses underneath.

The last MacLeod to live there is said to have been one Alistair Crotach (the hump-backed), who got a charter of Glenelg from James V in 1539. He left the castle after his child fell over the crags and was killed; and shifted his home to Dalla-mhor. Dalla-mhor became the site of the Free Church manse.

There are two other ancient structures on the Glenelg hills in the same vicinity—one above Galltair on the path over the hills to Ardintoul, the other above the military road near the Cnoc Mor. They are the Baghan Burblach (*burblach* is the name of an old farm) and the Baghan Galldair or Galltair. The Galltair baghan is the smaller of the two. Both are oblong enclosures with thick walls and remains of huts inside, and are placed on knolls. They have never been excavated. There is an Irish word *Badhun* which means an enclosure for cows, and these two Glenelg Baghans may have been a place in which animals could be shut for safety.

The line of the drove road goes on, through Glenelg and along the seashore, with a distant glimpse of the mountains of Rum and the level flat of Eigg in the far distance. Then it bends away from the sea and goes up Gleann Beag (the Little Valley), turning from the head of this glen up the valley of the Allt Ghleann Aoidhdailean. There is a made road along the right-of-way as far as Balvraid; from there onward it is a track.

Gleann Beag is perhaps even greener than Glen More (the Big Valley) in which Glenelg lies. The grass is green, the woods are green, the river plashes over the pebbles through little fields or cascades through a gorge. Here a waterfall drops like lace over black rock into the main stream.

But Gleann Beag does not attract visitors by its greenness and its soft, warm breezes, but by its brochs. They come into view suddenly as one rounds a bend; first Dun Telve by the river, and then Dun Troddan on higher ground. In both brochs about a third of the wall still rises to a considerable height, and the details of the structures are well preserved. They might have been better still if part of the stones had not been taken to help build the barracks.

They were circular drystone towers with double walls: some 500 probable or certain broch sites are known in Scotland and the Isles. They are a peculiarly Scottish structure, built probably by a fresh wave of Celtic invaders, rather in the manner of the Norman castles, to dominate the native population. The finds in the brochs seem to show that the brochs were inhabited by about the first century A.D. and continued in use in the north till the fifth or sixth centuries.

Most brochs are found in the Isles and the northern mainland, but a few have been found in the Scottish Lowlands. There is one known site at Torwoodlee near Galashiels, for example.

Here, in Gleann Beag, you may enter by the doorway and see the checks and sockets which held the wooden door, and the little "guard room" in the thickness of the wall. In the wall, too, are the strange passages, which would run all the way round inside the thickness of the wall when the structure was complete. In Dun Telve, there is still a stair with 17 steps leading up to the first passage. The lower ones are roomy enough to hold men and stores, and their stones are more carefully finished off than the higher ones which are smaller. It seems that the passages were a kind of scaffolding: the slabs which form their roof could be stood upon to build the next section of double wall.

The broch-builders seem to have had a good eye for agricultural land, *vide* the rich green flats about these two brochs. There are remains of outbuildings outside Dun Telve, which were probably to house the cattle of the folk who lived in the castle.

Both Dun Telve and Dun Troddan have been excavated and are now preserved by the Office of Works. Cups of schist were found, whorls for spinning, iron slag, both hand-made and wheel-made pottery fragments, querns (of the rotary pattern), a yellow bead of vitreous paste, a small bronze ring, a curved object made of whalebone.

Inside Dun Troddan (inner diameter 28 ft.) were found the remains of eleven posts. These must have supported a roof, the back of which could rest on the ledge which runs round the inner wall at a height of six feet. Three hearths were also found—one above the other, and so of three different ages.

Dun Troddan's highest section of wall is 25 feet high, and contains remains of three galleries or passages; Dun Telve has four pasasges and part of a fifth.

Leaving these two brochs behind and going on up the glen to Balvraid, where the motor road ends and the track begins one comes to another broch. This is Dun Grùgaig or Dun Chonil—it has two names, and it sits on a high crag above the wooded ravine in which the burn flows. It is about ten minutes walking from Balvraid. This broch is very ruinous and only one small portion of wall still shows its original regular building. One passage can be seen in this, and there is apparently another underneath—for there is a strong "subterranean" smell coming up through the tumbled stones. The wall on the side toward the rising hill is about 15 feet thick.

This Dun Chonil is remarkable among brochs in that brochs are circular towers, and Dun Chonil is only a half-circle. This is because the deep rocky gorge is sufficient projection upon one side. Inside the half-circle of wall, there seems to be a suggestion of a complete inner circle of stonework, as if the builders had been determined to get a circle in somewhere! It must have formed the basis of some inside building. It has not been excavated.

The stones of these brochs, which are carefully faced, are

got locally from the numerous outcrops all round. Some of the basal blocks in Dun Telve are very large indeed and would need many hands to move them. They grade evenly upward, getting progressively smaller and smaller toward the top of the tower.

There are four brochs in Gleann Beag. One stood on the rising ground at the mouth of the glen, but there appears to be little left of it now.

There are several legends about these brochs. One related by Pennant, who visited them in 1772, says that they were built by one Teilba for her four sons, and that they are accordingly called the Caisteal Teilbah or Castles of Teilba. He quotes a Gaelic rhyme:

> My four sons a fair clan,
> I left in the strath of one glen:
> My Malcomb, my lovely Chonil,
> My Telve, my Troddan.

Another legend concentrates upon Dun Telve and Dun Troddan and relates how they were built by the two Fingalian giants, Rhea and Akin. One stood beside a mountain about a mile away and passed the stones he picked up to the second giant, who set them in place! Rhea is said to have been drowned in Kyle Rhea, which bears his name, when he was jumping across. Kyle Akin is named after Akin. One or both giants were said to have been buried on a plain near Kyle Rhea, called the Imear nam Fear Mora, where there was a large barrow. Superstition believed that a terrible fate would overtake anyone who dared to disturb the grave. However, in the 1830's, some gentlemen did dig into and found two cists. These cists contained very large human bones—the jaw-bone could be easily fitted outside the jaws of one of the party; but they soon crumbled. Further excavation was stopped by a heavy thunderstorm, which the people regarded as a judgment on the excavators. However, eventually some bold spirit began

LOCH HOURN

The head of the fiord from Kinlochhourn, where
the cattle road from the Isles to the Great Glen
and the South starts to climb over the hills to
Glen Elg.

to plough the land and the site of the barrow passed almost out of memory.

Incidentally, Kyle Akin is certainly not called after any giant, but after King Hakon. He came to that part of the coast just before the battle of Largs.

The Reverend Alexander Beith, in the new *Statistical Account of Scotland* for Glenelg parish (1836), says that a subterranean passage led from Dun Telve to Dun Troddan and also to the river. This seems to be rather in the nature of legend, for he goes on to say that it was never explored. Something there must have been, for he says that the mouth was closed up because sheep and cattle fell into it; but where it really led is another matter

The cattle road turns up Gleann Aoidhdailean at a place called Srath a'Chomair. Near this place, a small vein of galena (lead sulphide) is seen in the schists. A sample which was analysed is said to have contained $65\frac{1}{2}$ ozs. of silver to the ton of lead. The lead miners of Glenelg and Strontian were some of the best customers of an Inverness merchant whose accounts have been preserved—relating to the years 1715-52. "Black lead" or graphite was also mined at Glenelg, near the manse in Glen More, which Pennant tells us was abandoned because of the poverty of the ore.

The road climbs over the broad hollow of the Bealach Aoidhdailean (1,550 ft.) between the massive Beinn nan Caorach and Sgurr na Laire Brice, and descends through a wide open valley to the trees at the head of Gleann Dubh. Here a track branches off to Arnisdale, whence a road leads back round the coast to Glenelg. The drove road goes on, up again over the moors, past the little pool of Lochan Torr a'Choit, over the Allt a'Choire Reidh and into a steep little hollow, up which it climbs, to drop even more steeply down to Kinloch Hourn on the other side.

The Allt a'Choire Reidh has some remarkably fine water-

falls below the crossing of the drove road. It descends to Loch
Hourn in a deep narrow gorge, in which the water leaps over
vertically bedded schists in a series of long cascades separated
by deep, dark pools.

The final rise above Kinloch Hourn is a place at which to
pause and look back. All the route from the Bealach is spread
out behind. At the head of the drop down to Kinloch Hourn
one can leave the track and look into the tremendous hollow
of Loch Hourn, and also up the glen at its head, where the
road to Glen Garry snakes like a white rope amongst grey rocks.

Loch Hourn and Loch Nevis are supposed to be the two
finest sea lochs or fiords in Scotland. They are long, deep,
winding arms of the Atlantic, above which rise great steep-
sided mountains. These fiords are regarded as the submerged
ends of valleys, which have been overdeepened by the action
of the ice sheets during the Glacial period. Both Hourn and
Nevis show, in a very marked fashion, a broad seaward portion
which is separated by a narrow and shallow channel, from a
narrow upper loch.

Hourn has many little islands. It is commonly called the
lake of Hell, whilst Nevis is the lake of Heaven. Indeed,
driving down the road from Glen Garry to Kinloch Hourn,
one does get the impression of descending into a great gash in
the surface of the earth, and the consideration of how ever to
get out again comes rather prominently to the fore.

As a matter of sober fact, Hourn does not mean hell, any-
more than Nevis means heaven. It is really Loch Shubhairne.
The burn coming down from the valley into the loch is the
Allt Coire Shubh—the burn of the corry of fruits or berries.
The gap or glen in which it flows is Subh-bhearna—the berry
gap and Loch Shubhairne is the lake of the berry gap. The
Gaelic pronunciation of the spelling *shubhairne* approximates
to the English way of saying *hourn*. The name Nevis seems to
have a more hellish than heavenly implication, for it seems to

mean the venomous one! The name Nevis is shared by the ben, the glen below the ben, and the sea loch on the west coast, some distance from Ben Nevis.

Coming to Kinloch Hourn in July I was puzzled by two things. The tide was out, and the scent of the yellow tangle was heavy on the still air. The loch water was a vivid blue-green, edged with the yellow spread of seaweed; then came a fringe of pink and above that the green meadows at the head of the loch. The pink from the distance, I thought was beach, but going down to it, found a great carpet of sea pinks (thrift) which spread all round the head of the loch. With it, playing a rather minor role in the colour scheme, was pink sea milk-wort.

The other curious sight at Kinloch Hourn are the trees with grey foliage which mingle with pines about Kinloch Hourn lodge, through the grounds of which the right-of-way runs. Fine trees they are, with straight grey stems, and while the frost of the spring of '47 had taken the rhododendrons and the heather and the gorse, these trees looked perfectly happy and at home; they are eucalyptus. The bamboo also lives in that district, I was told. All round rise very high and rugged and Scottish-looking mountains. The grey cloud of eucalyptus at their feet is the strangest thing in Kinloch Hourn.

CHAPTER VIII

THE ROUGH BOUNDS

I T is more exciting to go down to Loch Hourn from the heights of the Berry Corry—Coire Shubh—than to climb up from the sea as the Isles cattle must have done. Descending —the summit is 718 feet above sea level—one seems to pitch down into a deep green cleft in the mountains, the road dropping like the stream in sudden leaps down the rocks. The steepest grade is 1 in 6; the general grade 1 in 9.

Roads, whether one walks or whether one drives, have a curious effect of appearing steeper on the descent, and the Kinloch Hourn road is no exception. Going down, it seems so steep that the ascent appears almost impossible; the return journey, in fact, is a mere matter of one or two very steep sections, where the road is snuggled in between the gorge of the burn and the rocks above, and intervening, longer stretches of winding and climbing, but not very steep track.

In the more level stretches lie two little tarns, now very much silted up, and edged by reeds. The lower one, Loch Coire Shubh, has two monkey-puzzle trees planted one on each side of it, and looking rather out of place though extremely healthy.

At the top of the hill, where the cleft of the valley lies below with Loch Hourn hidden in its folds, is a little ruined building. It is made of undressed, rounded boulders of stone gathered locally; inside opposite the door, is a fireplace. This building was one of the old stage-houses on the road to Lochaber.

The rocks at the top of the gap are intensely smoothed. The ice travelled westward through the gap and rubbed the gneissic schists as it went, so that now they lie like great sheep amongst the hills, grey rounded ridges. On the other side, against the direction of the ice flow, each ridge is sharply cut off with a vertical face, for there the ice riding over the rock could not work in close to smooth the rock. Looking at the rock outcrops against the direction of the ice-flow, one sees all these dark slabby faces, rising tier upon tier up the hillside, like the ends of gigantic coffins.

The way goes down again, past more little reedy lochs, with high rocky hills upon either hand, to Loch Quoich—the Great Cup. This beautiful stretch of water is indeed a cup, a pool amongst great mountains, beside which grow ancient pines, and about Glenquoich Lodge, rhododendrons.

It is this district, whose mountains on the west lead over to Loch Hourn and Loch Nevis, on the north to Cluanie, and on the south to Loch Arkaig, that is called the Rough Bounds; rough in the Gaelic sense of crags and wild ravines, of waterfalls and lonely lakes.

From the bridge over the river Quoich, which enters the loch about its middle stretch, a right-of-way crosses the high mountains of Cluanie Forest by the Bealach Duibh Leac (Pass of the black flagstones) and comes steeply down into Glen Shiel. This was the way General Monck marched on the way to Kintail. It was also a coffin road. Prince Charles went over it in his wanderings after Culloden.

Just at the bridge, to the north, are two gravestones. They mark the resting place of two pedlars who were murdered in a nearby bothy. The 2,111-ft. hill above is called Bac na Ceannaiche—the ridge of the pedlars. This is one version of the name; the Ordnance map spells it Bac nan Canaichean which is more probably correct and would mean the ridge of cotton grass. Cotton grass is sometimes called mountain down.

The road is now running through the upper part of Glen Garry. Loch Quoich drains into Loch Garry, to which it is linked by a broad stream which snakes through green flats in a green valley, its course here and there broadening into a small loch, or enfolding a flat green island. Loch Garry in turn drains into Loch Oich in the Great Glen, and Loch Oich into Loch Ness, whose outflow is into the Moray Firth on the East Coast. Here, therefore, the headwaters of the East Coast rivers rise only two or three miles from the West Coast sea. The Loch Hourn-Loch Garry hollow is, of course, one of the cross-country through valleys.

The drove road to Lochaber and the Great Glen forded the river just above the head of Loch Garry. Here the slopes across the valley are so green that the farm upon the opposite side is called Greenfield, or in Gaelic, Ach' Uaine. Green hill-slopes are a feature of the whole way through from Loch Quoich, however; the rich summer grazing about that loch used to be shared out between the herds of Loch Hourn, Kintail and Glen Garry.

Just above the Greenfield ford is Eilean na Cloinne—the Children's Island. There eight children are said to have been left to play, when a strange monster came out of the water. It was a water-bull. The children immediately wanted to ride on its back and seven of them clambered on, but the eighth, more canny, first touched the creature's side with his finger. He found he could not withdraw the finger again! Seizing up a nearby sickle, he cut off the finger, and alone survived to tell the tale, for the beast, with a roar of rage, plunged below the water again, with the seven children on its back. Later, their seven hearts were found floating on the river.

These water-kelpy legends are very common in the Highlands. Sometimes the creature is an Each Uisge or water-horse. Some stories relate how the water-horse could be captured and used to plough and so forth, provided a bucket of water was poured over it night and morning. More often, the white horse stood ready saddled and bridled on the lochside waiting for the unwary to mount, after which neither were seen again! Or the water-horse might take human form in order to gain its victim.

Perhaps the story of the water-bull—the Tarbh-aighre, is connected with a memory of the wild white cattle which used to haunt the rich lochside pastures. More likely it is some remnant of ancient belief in the savage spirits which dwelt in lakes and mountains and springs. Sometimes the water-bull mated with ordinary cattle, its offspring being known by being Torc-chluasach—fork-eared.

Another unpleasant creature to meet on a dark night was the Bean-nighe, the washerwoman. She was usually seen pounding at her washing in the vicinity of dangerous fords and crooning to herself, *'Si do leine, 'si do leine ta mi nigheadh* ('Tis thy shroud, 'tis thy shroud, that I am washing). Needless to say, the victim of the vision died shortly afterwards.

The country in which the cattle road from Glenelg to Lochaber runs was, after the '45, kept well patrolled by the military, and the reports of the various officers in command are very interesting. There were, of course, the large barracks at Fort Augustus and Glenelg, but there were also many small posts set up about the glens, and moving patrols kept up between them to keep the Highlands in order. These patrols went along the various hill paths and drove roads, which would then be in more regular use and better condition than they are now. But the troops found the going terribly rough. Here is Captain Corneille of Colonel Herbert's Regiment, reporting from the station at the head of Loch Arkaig (where the barrack ruins can still be traced), on 11th July 1749:

Those detachments from Bernera (Glenelg), are pretty well supplyed with Necessaries. Glenmorrisson, I have not yet heard from, which I imagine, is owing to the rains we have had these two

F

days past. The other parties do not Complain, I cannot say much in praise of this situation, for the people in this part of the country are very poor, two or three Sheep, with as many Cows, is the richest man's stock, which they reserve for their own use, But I shall either send to fort William, or if possible nearer Hand for a supply. The Country is at present very quiet, And from the talk of those few I have spoken with, they seem pleas'd at their revolution, And I believe will gradually shake of that Servitude they shew'd to their Chiefs. The Cross ways from party to party are almost Impassable to our Men, tho as yet they have struggled through with Cheerfulness; I beg leave to observe that three or four days patroling wears out a pair of shoes.

There were small stations at the head of Glen Moriston, on the crossing between Loch Quoich and Loch Garry, at the head of Glen Shiel, at the head and foot of Loch Arkaig, at Strontian, in Morar and many other places. The network also covered the Highlands south of the Great Glen.

The troops took a lot of trouble rounding up people wearing the kilt, and were very annoyed when the local magistrates let the offenders off, with whom they naturally sympathised. The law was evaded by making out that the garment was not a plaid but a dyed blanket, not a man's kilt but a girl's, and so on. A particularly funny incident was duly reported from Loch Arkaig on 24th September 1750:

Ensign Irving reports that in his patrole he mett nothing extra— only saw two men with Phillibegs on, whom he persued, but they getting into a Hutt, mixing with others and Dropping the Phillibeg before he could get in, he could not prove who wore that Dress, however in order to Terrify them he seiz'd on two men, pinion'd them and march'd them away prisoners, and after some time dismiss'd them as he had no Proof.

The patrols certainly worked hard in their cross-country marches, as anyone who tries to follow in their footsteps will soon find out. Here is a report of one of Ensign Irving's patrols, dated 11th June 1750:

Ensign Irving who Commands the Moving patrole, has been his Circuit by the following post, Viz^t, from Glen Leogh up Arkaig side to the head of the Loch Arkaig. From thence thro' Glen Dissery along the side of Loch Morra, to Tray in Morra, from thence thro' Glen Dissery and Glen Pain, to Glen Finnan, from thence by Loch Sheil, to the Head of Loch in Dolet and to Strontian, from thence thro' Glen Tarbot to the Current of Argour and along Lochaber side to Glen Leogh, and found all well.

The moving patrol consisted in this district of one subaltern, one sergeant, one corporal and twenty men. The little posts had anything from four to fifteen men with one or two non-commissioned officers.

Lieut. Maxwell from Tray, in Morarr, informs me, he has made several attempts since last Report to send out Patroles, but they were prevented by the Snow and wth much difficulty returned to Quarters. He adds, that he is assured that it will not be in his Power to patrole any more this season. (5th November 1750, report from the Loch Arkaig station).

CHAPTER IX

THE OLD LADY OF FEDDEN

AT Greenfield, the droves had a choice of route. They might go between the hills in the narrow gap where stood the house of Fedden—wind whistle—down to Loch Arkaig, or they might cut across the shoulder of Ben Tee down to the Great Glen at Kilfinnan to join the Corrieyairack line of march, or go upon the north-west side of Loch Lochy to the foot of Loch Arkaig.

Rising from the smooth green slopes about Greenfield is the cone of Ben Tee—the Fairy Hill—and back of it, the great ridges of the Sron a'Choire Ghairbh and Meall na Teanga, which are separated from each other by the deep narrow gap of the Cam Bealach.

It is a long steady rise from Greenfield up to the "wind-whistle" gap, with a broad view back to the wooded hollow of Glen Garry. The way enters the pass, a green cleft between the Ben Tee–Sron a'Choire Ghairbh–Meall na Teanga bloc and the Meall na h-Eilde–Glas Bheinn hills on the other side. Meall na Teanga shows a red, scree-hung ridge to the north, falling to green corries from which streams cascade to the Allt Cam Bhealaich. Meall an Tagraidh is a round cone at the end of the Cam Bealach—the twisted pass—and below it stands Fedden house, a ruin now, once the highest inhabited house in the Glengarry lands. The drove road passes it and goes down the narrow green hollow of Gleann Cia-aig to the woods above the foot of Loch Arkaig, where the stream falls in silver ribbons over gnarled gneisses overhung by slender birch trees.

The Fedden crossing is on the east-west watershed parting of Scotland. A little to the north lies the marshy pool of Lochan Fhudair, which is interesting in that it lies exactly on the watershed. Its main outflow is to Glen Garry and the East Coast drainage; but some water seeps southward too, to the West Coast.

Here on the watershed is the boundary between Glen Garry and the Lochiel country. It is marked by a stream coming down the hill at one point, which by digging carefully, one can divert either to the one side or the other. This the old woman of Fedden, Cailleach na Fedden used to do. Her house lay beside the stream and whenever Glengarry's rent collectors called, the burn duly flowed upon their side of her house and she smilingly pointed out that she lived upon Lochiel's land. When Lochiel's men called for their rent, the burn was quietly running on the other side of the house, and the old lady was a supporter of the house of Glengarry!

The lower parts of Gleann Cia-aig are the most beautiful portions of the drove road here, where the glenside falls steeply to the rocky burn and the birches rise tier on tier above the young firs of the Forestry Commission. In the crags, where a branch track goes off just before the final drop to Loch Arkaig, was one of Prince Charles' hiding places. Here he hoped to meet Locheil but the latter was not fully recovered from his wounds and had to send his brother, Dr. Cameron, in his stead. From Loch Arkaig, the party moved on into Lochaber, to join Lochiel and Cluny MacPherson in Cluny's country. The place commands a wonderful view of Ben Nevis and the great range of the Lochaber mountains.

Loch Arkaig, with its ancient pine woods on its southern shores and those of birch and oak upon the north, is one of the most beautiful lakes in the Highlands. The drove road from Glenelg comes in below the foot of the loch and turns down the tree-clad gorge called the Dark Mile (Mile Dorcha) to

reach the Great Glen and Lochaber, Another drove road,
however, goes along the side of Loch Arkaig. This one comes
from Morar, and was important in the days when the Morar
folk took their cattle to sell at the Muir of Ord market. They
came either down Glen Pean or Glen Dessary to the head of
Loch Arkaig; then along the north shore of the loch, through
the Dark Mile; turning up along the north-west side of Loch
Lochy to Kilfinnan and Invergarry; then by Fort Augustus to
the old inn under Mealfuarvonie on Loch Ness and up through
Ruskich Wood to Glen Urquhart, and then more or less along
the line of the present road from Milton, over the hills to
Beauly and Muir of Ord.

The modern road along Loch Lochy goes along the south-
east shore; but the old track, along which Charles fled after
Culloden, on the other side, is perhaps one of the finest bridle
paths in Scotland. It is well maintained, with a good surface
of beaten earth along which one can walk easily and quickly.
The smaller fords have their bottoms built up with faced stones,
though the larger ones, where the force of water is greater,
are more irregular and might be difficult in spate. There are
never any of the doubts which so often assail the wanderer on
old tracks and rights-of-way: Is this the track or that? Where
does it go from here?—and so on. The way is firm and secure,
climbing not too much but winding about enough for variety;
a way through the young plantations of the Forestry Commission along the shore of Loch Lochy, where the blue water
laps on deep yellow beaches and across which the view is back
to the mighty cliffs of Ben Nevis with the snow still flecking
them through all the summer.

Here the influence of the Great Glen fault on the scenery
is very marked. The fault runs along the line of the long,
narrow Loch Lochy. The maximum depth of this lake is 531
feet; the average depth 229 feet. Across the water, rise the
green smooth slopes carved out of Dalradian schists—the schists

which build up so much of the southern Highlands. Graphite was once mined among them in this district. Across the line of faulting, the schists belong to the Moine series and are much harder, giving rise to rugged crags and higher peaks of more varied shape. The young fir plantations climb up the steep slopes, at the foot of which runs the track, with the youngest trees near the top. Above them come native birches and then the red heather and green turf with the grey rock breaking through it.

The streams come leaping down in straight courses from the craggy heights. Since little peat can exist on such hilltops, the water is crystal clear and sparkling, and the stream bottoms are seen through the limpid water as a pattern of grey and red and silver pebbles. Myself, I fancy that some of the ups-and-downs of the track are due to these very streams, that the way is in looking for good crossing places. Sometimes it goes over on the flat rock at the head of a waterfall.

Across Loch Lochy, the rhododendron bushes in the grounds of Invergloy House sit like round pink tuffets on the green turf; whilst upon this side, the smell of gorse mingles with that of hot brackens. Farther on, by a long-ruined house, there are gnarled hawthorns, thick with white blossom and patches of nettles which ever follow the habitations of men. Farther on still, at Glas-dhoire, there is a cottage still with a sagging roof of grey slate, where gooseberries and black currants and a clump of rhubarb still survive in the patch of garden outside. By the old houses, too, there are rowans, which keep away evil spirits, and holly and wild roses; whilst along the track grow bog asphodels, yellow bog pimpernel, blue and purple milkwort, butterwort, buttercup, bird's foot trefoil, marsh orchids, both the round and long-leaved sundews.

When Prince Charles sped from Culloden Moor, he came to Invergarry on the morning after the battle; going on by Loch Lochy in the afternoon to Loch Arkaig, where he sheltered for the night with Donald Cameron of Glen Pean. The old track would have been very different. There would have been more houses along it; the woods would have been naturally sown ones, and Loch Lochy would not have been so close to the track. For when the Caledonian Canal was made, the level of Loch Lochy was raised some eleven feet.

The raising of the level of the loch meant the disappearance of Eilean Darach, the oaken island, in Clunes Bay near Bun Arkaig, where the old track turns off up the lakeside. Clunes Bay also was largely done away with.

Eilean Darach was probably a natural island which was enlarged by art. It is said that the island was made in 1580 by Lachlan Mor Mackintosh to subdue the Lochaber men. However, the island was eventually broken down and the Lochaber men returned to their usual violent habits. The island is shown on the map (made in 1804) of the proposed route for the Canal.

But a different story is told about the island in Loch Lochy in one of the papers in *MacFarlane's Geographical Collections*. Its probable date is 1630. It relates that my Lord Cumming

builded ane Illand or ane house on the southeasthead of Loghloghlie with four bigg oak Jests that were below in the water And he builded ane house thereupone and ane devyce at the entrance of the said house That whaine anie did goe into the house ane table did lye by the way, that when anie man did stand upon the end theroff going fordward that end wold doune and the other goe up and then the man woman or dog would fall below in the water and perish. This house being finished, the Lord Cuming did call the wholl tennants and Inhabitants of the Countrey to come to him to that house, And everie one that did come into that place did perish and droune in the water And it fortuned at last that a gentleman one of the tenants, who had a hound or dog in his companie, did enter the house, and the dog did fall efter his master this dog being white, and comeing above the water in another place by the providence of God, without the house, the remant tennants which were as yet on going into the house, perceiving this to be rather for their destructione and confusione of these which were absent from them than for their better furtherance, did remove themselves and flitt out of that pairt wherin they were for the tyme to preserve themselves with their lives out of that cruell Mans hands. But my Lord comeing to be advertised heiraf perceiving the countrie and tenants to be somewhat strong as yet, did goe away by night and his wholl Companie out of the Countrie, And never since came to Loquhaber. And when summer is, certaine yeares or dayes, one of the bigg timber Jests the quantitie of ane ell therof, will be seen above the water and sundrie men of the countrie were wont to goe and see that Jest of timber q^ch stands there yet, And they say that a man's finger will cast it to and fro in the water, but fourtie men cannot pull it up because it lyeth in another Jest below the water.

It is possible to cross from the lochside track to Fedden by the magnificent Cam Bealach, a narrow cleft in the hills, which rises to almost 2,000 feet and on whose summit grow starry and yellow saxifrages, wild thyme and masses of alpine lady's mantle. The track over is fairly good all the way, except where the mountain torrents have swept through it and left behind a stony hollow.

Kilfinnan at the head of Loch Lochy is the graveyard where the chiefs of Glen Garry lie buried. They were carried over the hills from Glen Garry to the little graveyard on the southern band of the Kilfinnan burn. Here, too, came down the other branch of the drove road from Greenfield. Kilfinnan means, of course, the church of Finan, who came of the race of Oilill Olum of Munster. "Ane Idolatrous Image called St. Finane" was duly burned at Inverness market cross in 1643, after it had been discovered preserved in a private house.

Glen Garry had a number of ancient burying grounds. In later days, Glen Garry folk were buried in Glen Moriston at Achlain, as has already been described. Their chiefs and other MacDonells rest at Kilfinnan, after a fairly long cross-country carry. But in Glen Garry itself are two old burying grounds— one at Greenfield and the other at Kildonan. Donnan was martyred in Eigg in A.D. 617. His day is 17th April. Kil, Gaelic *cille* means a church. There is an old saying:

> *Cill Fhinn's Cill Duinn's Cill Donnain,*
> *Na tri cilltean as sine an Albainn.*

> Killin, Kildun and Kildonan,
> The three oldest churches in Scotland.

Above Kilfinnan on the moorland plateau from which Ben Tee springs, is the little tarn of Lochan Diota, where the white water lilies grow and the view reaches far up the Great Glen, where Loch Ness lies amongst the high hills like a narrow mirror. Beside the Loch is a jumbled pile of schist blocks, and here the funeral parties often rested. Once a quarrel broke out amongst the mourners and a corpse was carried back to Glen Garry by the men who had started out in the morning with a different body. When they told the elderly woman who was the grandmother of the dead man and lived at Laddie in Glen Garry, she exclaimed, with some sarcasm, "My blessing on the Glen Garry men who will take one corpse out and bring another one home!"

Lochan Diota is called the Dinner Loch partly because funeral parties stopped there for a meal; but chiefly because here the MacDonells had their dinner before they intercepted the Frasers in the Great Glen at Achadrom where they fought the famous battle of the shirts. This was fought in 1544. The MacDonells each placed a stick in the ground at the Dinner Loch before going forward, so that they would be able to count their losses on their return. The battle of Blar na Leine was very fierce—the Frasers were wiped out almost to a man and the MacDonell party nearly so. The Frasers fought in their shirts, throwing aside their heavy plaids, thus giving rise to the name of the battle.

Laggan Achadrom was also the site of one of the principal military posts after the '45. The name Achadrom means the field of the ridge; the ridge is the ridge of Scotland, which separates the eastward from the westward flowing streams. Laggan means a hollow. There used to be a stone marking the exact summit of the ridge. Here there was held a fair, and here too were the local gallows. The old deeds relating to the neighbouring country were all signed here. The place was also the site of the first skirmish between the Prince's forces and the British troops, when some English regulars were caught between a party of MacDonells of Keppoch coming up from the west, and the Kennedies of Laggan.

It is possible to encircle Ben Tee, Sron a'Choire Ghairbh and Meall na Teanga by following these old tracks round, or to make a shorter circuit by using the Cam Bealach, and it is quite an interesting, if lengthy, walk. But the way over the moor from Kilfinnan to join the drove road coming from Greenfield to Fedden is simple bog walking, with no track at all, and the round should therefore be begun from Kilfinnan to get this bad section over first. The views from the moor there are, however, extremely fine, both along the Great Glen and up Glen Garry.

V

THE ROAD THE SOLDIERS MADE

CHAPTER X

FORT AUGUSTUS TO GLENELG

"To a party to work upon the road leading from Fort-Augustus to Bernera and the island of Sky, which party to consist of 2 Subaltern officers, 92 days, at 3s. each per diem, 4 Sergeants at 1s. each, 4 Corporals at 8d. each, 2 Drummers and 100 men at 6d. each = £292 17s. 4d. Extraordinary charges for Artificers, carts, tools, lime, underground drains, coal and other incidental expenses, £239 10s. 0d." (*House of Commons Journal*, Vol. xxxii, p. 701).

The Military Road from Fort Augustus to Bernera Barracks at Glenelg was the principal military road made north of the Great Glen, for little work seems to have been done by the soldiers on the other military road in this area—that from Contin to Poolewe. The Glenelg road belongs to the series of new military roads made after the '45, and has no connexions with General Wade. The quotation above shows the rates of extra pay received by the men who worked on the roads. The full details of the construction of the road are lacking; it was in existence with men working on it when Johnson and Boswell traversed it in 1773, and it was probably begun somewhere about 1750 when work is known to have been in progress on it. It was abandoned in 1784, but the bridges were maintained till 1795, and probably later, by a mason named John of Strathdee. It is named in the detailed estimates given to Parliament from 1770 to 1784. The cost ranged from £532 7s. 4d. in the first year to £158 9s. 4d. in the last.

It is an extremely interesting road to travel, both because of the mountain scenery on either hand and because of its historical associations. It climbs straight over the ridge between Fort Augustus and Glen Moriston, which it reaches at Achlain, and for this first section is indistinct in many places. From Achlain onward, the present road more or less follows it, though the old road deviates from the modern line at a number of points in the Cluanie country. If the hydro-electric scheme for Loch Cluanie and Glen Moriston is completed, the present road will be submerged and a new line constructed more nearly on that of the old military road through that district.

Fort Augustus was originally called Kilcumein—Cummein's church. There may have been a fort built there by Cromwell; the first, of which there is a record dating from 1716, was on the site of the present Lovat Arms Hotel. General Wade began the building of a new fort in 1727, because he thought the old one too far from Loch Ness. It was Wade who gave the name of Fort Augustus. The old buildings of Wade's fort now form the basis of the present Benedictine monastery.

Wade's fort was finished in 1742 and surrendered to the Highland Army in February 1746, for which the commanding officer, Major Wentworth, was court-martialled. It was later the headquarters of the Duke of Cumberland and an important strong point in the Highlands.

There was apparently a much earlier castle belonging to the Cummings on the site of the present Abbey tower, and which was pulled down to make way for Wade's barracks.

Fort Augustus lies snug in the middle of the Great Glen—Glen More nan Albyn—the Great Valley of Scotland. The old road climbs sharply up the hillside to the ridge above Glen Moriston, taking the first steep slope under the rounded knoll of Creag Iarlain in a series of hairpin bends. The bends are built up on the outside, and near the top the way is cut through the living rock. This way came Dr. Johnson and Mr. Boswell en route for Skye and it is amusing to catch Dr. Johnson, normally very much the sceptic, enjoying the hairpin bends like a school boy. He writes: "We soon came to a high hill, which we mounted by a military road, cut in traverses, so that as we went upon a higher stage, we saw the baggage following us below in a contrary direction."

Undoubtedly the best time to see this part of the old road is in winter. A light fall of snow rests more level on the track than on the heather alongside and shows the way up as a white ribbon snaking over the brown moor. But the unwary should beware of a light fall of powder snow on this road. Many springs course down it and after frosts, the way becomes a solid path of ice. Powder snow hides these stretches of ice, but affords no grip on them, so that the walker is suddenly sent off at a furious pace downhill with little prospect of remaining for long on his feet. After the snow has frozen to the ice, the going is very good under winter conditions.

Climbing toward the ridge, the view spreads wide behind. Fort Augustus lies clustered in the valley; Loch Ness sparkles in the sun, with the crannog Cherry Island sitting like a ship in Inchnacardoch Bay. Across the glen is the green valley leading up to the rolling uplands of Corrieyairack, with Cullachy House standing a grey pile on green grass amongst the trees of the Tarf valley. The reconstructed line of Wade's road to Inverness curls up Glen Doe hill; Beinn a'Bhacaidh of the silver crags rises leonine from Loch Ness. Westward, the Ben Tee group springs up from the moors, and across the Great Glen the view is straight into the northern corries of Ben Nevis. Immediately below lie the neat plantations of the Forestry Commission on the level plain of the King's Moor—the Blar an Righe. The crags rise sudden from the moor upon the north-west side, and on a little out-jutting knob of gneiss is Torr Dhuin.

G

Torr Dhuin is a vitrified fort, now thickly encircled by Forestry plantations. But one can still see the outline of wall, where the heat of fire has melted the stones of which it is built, so that vitrified rock is the cement between them. Torr Dhuin is one of a chain of such vitrified forts which sit on commanding positions along the Great Glen, and which are supposed to have communicated with one another by beacon fires. The other known vitrified forts along the glen are Craig Phadrig at Inverness, Castle Urquhart, Dun Deardail, Inverfarigaig and Dun Deardail, Glen Nevis. Dun Scriben above Ruskich Wood, Loch Ness, has also been said to be vitrified, but I can find no evidence to support this statement. There are also said to be vitrified forts at Dores and Corran Narrows.

Vitrified forts are found in many parts of Europe as well as in the Scottish Highlands. They date from the early Iron Age, and they are earlier than the brochs.

It seems that the Celts who built them constructed the Gallic walls which Caesar described in Gaul. These were made of stone bonded together with vertical and horizontal logs; the core included many small rubble stones which helped to prevent the logs rolling out of place. If such a wall catches fire, part of the wood is first converted into charcoal. When this charcoal burns, the heat produced is sufficient to fuse the rocks. The production of vitrifaction by burning a Gallic wall has been demonstrated experimentally.

Did the chiefs who lived in the forts set them alight deliberately, with the intention of having molten rock for cement? It seems in some cases that they certainly did not, for the melted wall has slumped onto various buildings inside the fort. But the accident might have given them an idea to carry out deliberate vitrifaction. Or it may be that the vitrified remains tell the tale of the overthrow of their owners either by the broch-building invaders or by the Romans.

Torr Dhuin I think is accidental vitrifaction. The vitrified wall appears to have slipped slightly over the edge of the crag and then solidified there. One could not build a wall in such a position, but a burning, sticky mass could easily slide down.

Torr Dhuin is the first of the vitrified forts to have been described: it was first mentioned by Pennant who visited it on 1st September 1769. This is his description of the fort, which then was not so well masked by trees as it is now.

Rode to the castle of Tor Down, a rock two miles West of Fort Augustus: on the summit is an antient fortress. The face of this rock is a precipice; on the accessible side is a strong dyke of loose stones; above that a ditch and a little higher, a terrace supported by stones; on the top a small oval area, hollow in the middle: round this area, for the depth of near twelve feet, are a quantity of stones strangely cemented with almost vitrified matter, and in some places quite turned into black scoria: the stones were generally granite, mixed with a few grit stones of a kind not found nearer the place than 40 miles. Whether this was the antient site of some forge, or whether the stones which form this fortress had been collected from the strata of some Vulcano (for the vestiges of such are said to have been found in the Highlands) I submit to farther enquiry.

Below the fort lies the graveyard of Kilmalomaig. It is named after St Moluag, whose headquarters were in the Island of Lismore in Loch Linnhe, and who died in A.D. 592. Here rests Allan MacRanald of Lundy—he of the fight under Meal-fuarvonie.

I heard a good story concerning this graveyard. A funeral party came over the hill from Glen Moriston, divided into two companies, of which the first carried the body. The way was long and the corpse was heavy and on the top of the ridge, the first party decided to leave the coffin for the second party to carry down. The second party went gaily on, and the company met at Kilmalomaig without the body. One can imagine the feelings of the mourners who had to climb back up the hill again to look for the body!

Three stones standing by the way as the road climbs on and

up are called the Wedding Stones. Here Glen Moriston folk
trysted with the Fort Augustus minister to be married; bap-
tisms are also said to have been conducted there.

It is now a long steady pull to the moorland ridge, from
which the view opens out to Glen Moriston. The streams are
crossed by some beautiful little stone bridges which still remain in a good state of repair. Various depressions along the
way show where road metal was dug, or where rock was got
for the bridges.

On the summit stand a small group of funeral cairns, and a
deeply stained spring comes bubbling up. It is the Fuaran Ruadh
—the Red Spring. Its colour is due to iron deposits in the peat
through which it rises. It is certainly not a spring from which
to take a long drink!

The road runs gently down to Achlain. The bridge over
the Allt Phocaichain (Burn of the Sacks) is down and the
crossing might be difficult in times of rain. The road is very
indistinct at this point, and the drove road which branches off
from it to go down to Torgyle bridge, almost lost.

Beside the track here grow fine Scots pines and silver
birches; a small scrap that is left of the old Dalcattack Forest.
This forest was mainly pine upon the Glen Moriston side, and
oak and birch upon the Loch Ness side. Some of the trees
were at least 150 years old. The firs were sold and felled
about the time of the first World War. There is a record in
1665 of a ship being built by Lord Lovat at Inverness of Dalcattack oak and fir. This ship was the biggest that had ever
been seen in those parts.

The fir wood, when cut into splinters, burned well enough
to light the Glen Moriston houses of an evening, and a gangrel
tramp might earn his night's rest by keeping the splinters
burning, lighting one from the other as it burned down. There
is a saying: "Glen Moriston, where the dogs will not eat the
candles"!

The inscription on Roderick Mackenzie's Cairn

Roderick Mackenzie's Cairn in Glen Moriston

Fine native pines stand on the moors at intervals all the way up Glen Moriston to Loch Cluanie, especially about Ceannacroc and the river Loyne.

The track joins the modern road at Achlain, and some way farther on, where it turns over a small bridge over a burn is a sheep fank. It was here that Dr. Johnson stopped the night en route for Skye, and was so impressed by the culture of the daughter of the house that he presented her with a book which he happened to have with him—*Cocker's Arithmetic*. Here, too, came the soldiers which Johnson had seen working on the road and given 2s. each—"as we were enjoying the benefit of their labours". Johnson later gave them another shilling each and they became very much the worse for drink and there was some fighting before the night was past.

Aonach Inn was built by the British Government at a cost of £80 in 1770. Next year, various offices and stables were erected at a cost of £60 5s. Boswell says it was built of turves and that there were three rooms in line and a smaller room projecting out. The inside was lined with plaited wattles. For dinner, Johnson and Boswell had chicken, mutton chops, mutton sausage and eggs. Johnson ate five eggs but nothing else. Rum was available and water and sugar, the party had brought their own lemons and made lemonade for Johnson. Boswell contrived to eat four eggs, some chicken and some sausage, as well as drinking rum.

As the road approaches Ceannacroc, with its big shooting lodge, there stands a cairn by the wayside. It was here that Roderick MacKenzie, the son of an Edinburgh jeweller was killed. He bore a striking resemblance to Prince Charles and being mistaken for him, was set upon by a party of soldiers. Roderick died defending himself and the illusion, crying out as he fell: "You have murdered your Prince." His head was removed for identification, and the delay while this was done probably saved Charles.

Ceannacroc means the Knoll of the Heads. The story of the origin of the name tells of a battle between the Gordons under the Marquis of Huntly and the Camerons under Lochiel. The Gordons were defeated and Huntly taken prisoner. Just when all seemed lost, Mac-Ian-Chaoil and his men, came to the rescue. Mac-Ian-Chaoil was the chief of a sept of MacDonalds who lived in Glen Moriston and many of whom are buried at Achlain which, incidentally, is one of the oldest graveyards in the country.

The Camerons retreated before the fresh onslaught, but took with them seven Gordon prisoners. Finding the men a drag on their escape, they beheaded them on the Knoll of the Heads.

The Battle of the Braes of Glenmoriston may have been fought during the final stages of Huntly's rising in 1647, when Huntly was overtaken by General Middleton who had some Camerons in his troup. Huntly managed to escape, but was captured later in the same year. But the legend is vague as to its date.

The way ahead is a long hard march. On either side rise the mountains, Sgurr nan Conbhairean to the north and Beinn Loine to the south, with the narrow loch of Cluanie cradled between them. In front, are the mountains of the ancient Royal chase of Cluanie. The road crosses the watershed and descends between Cluanie Forest upon the one hand and the Five Sisters of Kintail on the other.

They are tremendous mountains, lifting sheer above the narrow gorge. Dr. Johnson was not impressed. "Of the hills", he writes, "which our journey offered to the view on either side, we did not take the height, nor did we see any that astonished us with their loftiness."

Boswell was more willing to be impressed. He pointed out a mountain and said it was immense. Johnson contradicted at once: "No", said he, "but 'tis a considerable protuberance."

Boswell pointed out a mountain shaped like a cone (perhaps Faochag—the Whelk). "No, sir," said Johnson, "It would be called so in a book; and when a man comes to look at it, he sees 'tis not so. It is indeed pointed at the top. But one side of it is much longer than the other."

Now Johnson may not have been an acute observer in these matters—he had come the day before through Dalcattack Forest and yet claimed that the Highlands were quite treeless; but I think the mountains of Glen Shiel are not impressive until one has seen a great deal of mountain scenery. They tower too much over the road for their forms to be properly realised, and until one has learned to judge the scale of hills, they do not appear particularly high. To the mountaineer, they are a magnificent challenge; to the stranger from the lowlands they are merely hills upon either side of a deep gorge.

Sgurr Fhuaran (3,505 ft.), the chief amongst the Five Sisters, rises from the valley in one long slope of 3,500 feet, which is probably the longest continuous slope in the country. The spelling of the name is uncertain; some people write it Sgurr Oran—the Peak of the Song. Some 300 years ago, there was a great bagpipe contest in Kintail. The final test was to play the pipes all the way to the top of Sgurr Oran. Near the top, a Macrae was a little in front of the second man, who bent forward and slit the leader's bag with his dagger. The Macrae, however, managed to keep the pipes going till he sprang on to the summit, exclaiming "Sgurr Oran" and thus both naming the hill and giving the Macraes a war-cry. The Macrae crest is a bared right arm holding a dagger with the motto "Fortitudine".

Where the road plunges into a narrower part of the glen and crosses the river Shiel, was fought the Battle of Glen Shiel in 1719. This Jacobite rising, supported by a Spanish contingent, was a short-lived sequel to the '15. The Jacobite forces held the pass and were in an extremely strong position to

check the advance of the Government forces from the east.
A small party ought to have been able to hold the pass; in 1719,
the opposing forces were nearly equal. The Government troops
included some Highlanders who carried out an outflanking
movement on the hill sides, and General Wightman who com-
manded the party succeeded in putting the rebels to confusion.
Losses on the Jacobite side were very small; the Government
had 21 killed and 121 wounded. The Spaniards surrendered
after blowing up their ammunition dump at the Manse of Kintail.

The Battle of Glen Shiel—the date was 10th June and the
time 5 p.m.—is peculiar in being almost the only Highland
battle in which Highlanders were on the defensive and in which
there was very little hand-to-hand fighting.

In 1719, of course, the military road had not been made,
but General Wightman, who marched from Fort Augustus,
came more or less along its line. It is probable that there would
be a track there then. Maps earlier than the military road
show the hairpin bends over Mam Ratagain, and the route was
one along which cattle from Skye were driven south.

About a mile from Shiel, there is an underground "earth
house", lined with stone. The chamber is about eight feet
high, but the entrance is now closed up. In the vicinity of
Shiel, too, were found two inscribed stones put up by the
soldiers working on the road. One was found in place, about
two miles from Shiel Inn (now closed). It read: XXIV REG
ENDED. The other was found in the wall of a house on the
shore of Loch Duich and was more detailed: THE IV OR
KING'S OWN ROYAL REG. MADE 249 [? yards] OF ROAD
EA [st] 1771.

At Shiel, the road to Glenelg turns away from Loch Duich
and climbs over the Bealach Ratagain (1,116 ft.) to drop down
into Glen More. It is a great climb. The hillside is now well
wooded by the young pine plantations and the future move-

THE FIVE SISTERS AND LOCH DUI(

The Five Sisters of Kintail rise from Glen Shie
to the right of the picture ; behind them is th(
serrated ridge of Beinn Fhada and the opening

FROM MAM RATAGAIN SUMMIT

the Glens leading eastward to Glen Affric.
me of the twists of the Mam Ratagain road
e seen in the foreground.

ments of the stony little track are concealed to the climber. I got the impression of the road desperately casting about to try and find some way over the summit and up the steep hillside. The steepest gradient is 1 in 6, the average 1 in 12. The surface is loose enough for car wheels to skid in, and it is the roughness of the way which provides most of the difficulty in taking a vehicle up it. When the *New Statistical Account* was written in 1836, the minister of Glenshiel described the Mam Ratagain road as too steep for carriages.

The summit commands a very extensive view. It is now possible to see the Five Sisters of Kintail in proper perspective, and glimpse behind them Beinn Fhada and the mouths of the through valleys leading east into Glen Affric. Far below lies the green water of Loch Duich and the yellow coils of the road. Across the ridge, the mighty mountains about Loch Hourn rise to the south, and ahead is Skye, with the fantastic Cuillin Hills showing through a break in the nearer hills.

The descent to Glenelg is more gradual. Dr. Johnson, who had ridden all the way from Aonach, was, by this time, rather tired and peevish. It seemed a very long way down to the weary party. The horse hirer walked beside Dr. Johnson and tried to amuse him by remarks such as "See such pretty goats" and then whistling to make them jump away. Boswell "laughed immoderately" at his attempts.

The party could not put up at the barracks as there were only a few soldiers quartered there and had to make shift with the inn, such as it was. "They had no bread, no eggs, no wine, no spirits but whisky, no sugar but brown grown black." Boswell tells how they produced some mutton chops but the travellers would not take them; eventually a chicken was killed. Dr. Johnson, however, had his lemonade, for the factor of MacLeod, knowing the inn's circumstances, sent round some sugar as well as "a bottle of excellent rum".

The sleeping accommodation was equally poor, but after

the travellers had rejected the beds provided, some hay was got for them, which they spread on the ground. Dr. Johnson tells how he slept on the hay in his riding coat but that "Mr. Boswell being more delicate, laid himself sheets with hay over and under him, and lay in linen like a gentleman".

The shell of Bernera Barracks stands on the level pasture by the sea at the mouth of Glen More, a solid pile of grey stone. The date of the erection of the barracks is not certainly known; all that can be made out on the keystone over the entrance now is GR and 17. But according to accounts given by old people in Glenelg, the date on the stone was 1719. They were designed to hold 200 men, but, after the rebellion was over, were held by a small handful of men. The old *Statistical Account* for Glenelg, written in 1795, says that for the previous twenty years, there had only been a sergeant or a corporal and a few privates stationed there. They lived in the officers' quarters; the soldiers' quarters were already ruinous. The military seem to have left altogether about 1800. Later on, some poor families moved in, until such time as the factor chose to turn them out of the place by the expedient of burning the roof.

The ground about the barracks is "Grunnd an Righ"—the King's Ground; and the Glenelg folk still keep to the military order in their funerals, which they learned from the soldiers. In the neighbouring parishes the coffin is carried at the head of the procession, but at Glenelg it comes last.

VI

THE VERY OLD ROAD FROM THE WEST TO THE EAST

THE BEALACH AN SGAIRNE

" A small gap in the mountain, as if it had been sawn down to the middle "—the summit of the pass from Kintail to Glen Affric and Strath Glass.

CHAPTER XI

KINTAIL TO GLEN AFFRIC AND STRATH GLASS

Of the direct roads through the hills from west to east that of the Bealach an Sgairne (1,700 ft.) is perhaps the most ancient and the most interesting. It was over this track that some of the Celtic saints travelled. Loch Duich, from which the road leads, is named after St. Duthac. He must have used the pass when he travelled eastward to his church at Tain in Easter Ross. The Bealach an Sgairne is also called the Cadha Dhuich—St. Duthac's Pass. St. Duthac is said to have died at Armagh in 1065.

The route remained in use until the coming of wheeled vehicles to the Kintail country, when it was let out of use rather than be regraded.

The way leaves the shores of the sea loch Duich at a farm called Morvich and goes up a green valley to the croft of Innis a'Chro, turning northward to follow the south bank of the Amhainn Chonaig immediately the croft house is passed. It then turns up Gleann Choinneachain, crosses the Bealach an Sgairne and goes down Gleann Gniomhaidh into Glen Affric. From Glen Affric the way is open to the east through Strath Glass, or to the south, by joining the Poolewe-Fort Augustus route at Tomich.

The country about the head of Loch Duich, a land of high green hills and grey rocks, with rich pastures in the narrow glens, is Kintail—in Gaelic *Ceann an t-saile* (the head of the salt water). Here the fiord lochs snake up among the hills,

Alsh dividing into the narrow limb of Loch Long and the broader Loch Duich. Here amongst the high, quiet hills, the tide runs out leaving a wide spread of yellow seaweed, and boats glide across the glittering ripples to gather in the nets, which dry on rough frames about the crofts.

At the head of Loch Duich, a small headland juts out and on it stands the ruin of the old church of Kintail, which served the little township of Clachan Duich. Between the roofless walls, the chiefs of Clan Macrae are buried; for Kintail is Macrae country; and here, too, they say are buried some of the Spaniards who lent half-hearted help to the rising of 1719.

At the tip of the headland, there rises a round grassy knob. This is the site of the broch, Dunan Diarmaid. There now only remains to be seen the foundation of the broch, for the stones were taken to build the nearby house. When the old *Statistical Account* for the parish of Kintail was written in 1793, the broch walls stood twenty feet high. Beside it is the so-called grave of Diarmaid—Uaigh Diarmaid. This consists of twenty large stones forming a double parallel row, 27 feet long. In the old days, members of Clan Campbell, who claim to be descended from the Fingalian Diarmaid, used to come and measure the grave of their hero.

The traditional story of Diarmaid's death is this. The wife of the chief Fingalian, Fionn, was called Grainne, and fell in love with Diarmaid. They eloped together from Ireland and eventually came to Glen Elg. Fionn came hunting in the district and being hard pressed by a wild boar, shouted for help. Diarmaid came to the rescue and duly slew the beast. Fionn then asked him to measure it from tail to snout. While Diarmaid was doing this, his one vulnerable point—his heel, was scratched by a poisoned bristle, and he died. But there are many different versions of the story, nor do they all agree as to the place in which the various events occurred.

As the old road eastward turns up into the hills, one can

look back across Loch Duich to the twisting coils of the Mam Ratagain road to Glenelg. On the one hand, rise the end of the great ridge of mountains that make up the Five Sisters of Kintail; on the other, Sgurr an Airgid. Westward, Sgurr an Airgid slopes down to form the lower height of Beinn Bhuidhe, whilst opposite is another Beinn Bhuidhe—the end of the great ridge of Beinn Fhada. Beinn Bhuidhe means the Yellow Mountain; probably the two are distinguished by adding the name of the massif on which they occur, or by calling them north and south, but it is unusual to have two hills of the same name on either side of the same glen.

Beinn Fhada—the Long Mountain, is a great sharp-edged ridge of hill, which lies behind and parallel to the Five Sisters, from which it is separated by Gleann Lichd. The road to Glen Affric runs along the north flank of Beinn Fhada, but there is an alternative, though less important route, along the southern flank.

It is pleasant walking the old track from Innis a'Chro, round the Beinn Bhuidhe end of Beinn Fhada. In the hot sun the bog myrtle scents the soft air (there is a grove of monkey puzzles round Morvich Farm) and mingles with that of the honeysuckle which scrambles amongst the bushes lining the rocky gorge of the Amhainn Chonaig. Here the road has been surfaced with large boulders, laid cobblewise, so as to form a firm track through the wet ground.

There are still many cattle in Kintail, but perhaps not enough to justify its old nickname of Kintail no Bogh—Kintail of the Cows. "It is not size, but shape and figure, that gives the Kintail cattle the claim to preference, in the opinion of drovers, who always expect to meet with three good properties, a choice pile, weight, and short legs, in the true breed of cattle on the soil" (*Old Statistical Account*, Kintail, 1793).

The road turns eastward up the deep, green cleft of the Gleann Choinneachain—the valley of moss. It is a beautiful glen, very sheer sided, with the grassy slopes lifting to grey craggy heights of schist, down which pour clear torrents to join the burn which flows swiftly down the floor of the valley. The main stream runs in a rocky and narrow channel, overhung here and there by trees, and dropping in waterfalls into crystal pools, or vanishing over a ledge into some narrower and deeper cleft. The pools, faintly greenish, are so clear that every detail of their floors can be seen from the track on the valley side above.

In front, a rocky spur of Beinn Fhada—Meall a'Bhealaich (the round hill of the pass) and another craggy height of the northern flank of the valley—A Ghlas-bheinn (the grey mountain) 3,006 feet—are separated only by a narrow but deep cleft. The track ahead can be seen climbing up to this wind gap in a series of four hairpin bends and traverses. It is a well made little path for all this distance. Where it crosses streams which descend in straight deep channels, the channels have been properly filled up to make a level crossing, the water being allowed to flow over the top and form a shallow ford. The grading of the road is quite good, and it is gentle enough to walk steadily and quickly to the summit without making any undue effort. But it is worth pausing to look back, down the deep glen to the hills beyond its mouth—the brindled hill—Beinn Bhreac with its dappled line of ice-smoothed rocks; or to glance up the slopes of Beinn Fhada, where the Rough Corry—Choire Gairbh, cuts deeply into the mountain in a great arcuate crag.

The last stretch above the hairpin bends is very striking. There is a narrow dry valley cut through the Moine schists, which are here reared up on end, vertical. The valley is rocky and littered with boulders, amongst which grow saxifrages and wild thyme. Above the valley sides rise the two sentinel mountains which form the jaws of the pass. There are some attempts at making enclosures in the pass itself with the fallen stones, but whether they ever formed cattle folds, I do not know. On the top is a small cairn. One comes up to it and peeps over the top. The hillside falls more rapidly and the path goes down by a series of hairpins, more acute and numerous than on the west side. Below sparkles Loch a'Bhealaich (the loch of the pass), with two little islands upon its face. One island is much larger than the other and evidently natural; the other is a small round thing, which looks like an artificial crannog.

The description of the pass, the Bealach an Sgairne, given by the minister of Kintail in 1793 is interesting because at that time the way was in regular use. He wrote:

But of all the roads leading to this place (Kintail), none calls more for public attention than that of Afric or Belloch. This road is 13 computed miles from Kilduich in Kintail, to Knockfin in Strathglass. It is allowed to be the nearest communication between the east and west seas; and, though daily frequented by people from Sky and other places, to Inverness and Dingwall, with heavy loads, there is no inn to accomodate travellers, except the booths of shepherds, which in stormy weather they frequently burn for feul. Within 3 miles of Kintail, at a place called Belloch, is a high ridge of hills which environs this district on the east and would render it inaccessible from that quarter, if nature had not left a small gap in the mountain, as if it had been sawn down to the middle, which leaves room for 3 passengers to go abreast. The ascent on the east to the Belloch is about 100 yards in a zig-zag direction. The western aspect is truly steep and vexatious: the intermediate space on the top is a quarter of a mile long, and 5 feet broad. The traveller finds himself, in passing through this gut, in-closed with hills of rueful aspects, inspiring awe, and often quickening his pace.

It was by this route that Lord George Sackville came after Culloden, driving cattle and other plunder before him. The minister of Kintail, Mr. John M'Lean set off into the hills to intercept him and prevent the loyal Kintail people being rav-aged. Mr. M'Lean was very simply dressed and Lord George

H

refused to believe that he really was the minister. After some argument, he was ordered, at the point of the pistol, to produce his library as evidence of his identity. Mr. M'Lean went home and brought out *Pool's Annotations*—which had the necessary effect! The book was carefully preserved for some time after as a kind of heirloom.

Loch a'Bhealaich lies in the lap of the steep green hills. Its waters flow northward through a broad marshy strath to drop down into Glen Elchaig in the falls of Glomach. These falls are over 300 feet high and the longest in the country. As one comes down from the pass to the loch, the view is open down the wide strath to the drop to Glen Elchaig and to the hills beyond that glen to the north. On the other side of the loch rises Beinn Fhada, and the way opens down another broad grassy glen—Gleann Gniomhaidh. The humpy mounds of glacial gravels which lie between the lochside and the head of this glen form the watershed between east and west, for the Glomach burn drains into Loch Long on the west coast.

Loch a'Bhealach is a basin hollowed out of the solid rock by the passage of ice in the Ice Age. During the Ice Age the ice shed lay to the east of the present watershed. Ice thus drained over the low cols which lie on the watersheds in the old cross-country valleys and smoothed and moulded them into flats, in the hollows of which now lie tarns and lakes.

The track is lost in the bogs for a short stretch as it goes down Gleann Gniomhaidh, but it soon becomes clear again, running close to the stream on the north bank. It is now distinct right on to Loch Affric, five or six miles farther down the hollow. At Affric Lodge, it becomes a road proper. The country of Glen Affric has already been described in connexion with the Poolewe-Fort Augustus road, but it may be proper to point out here that the old route was not that of the present driving road. This was made when the shooting lodge on Loch Affric was built in 1870, and it was agreed that the proprietor

IN GLEN AFFRIC

On the Kintail-Strath Glass right of way near
Athnamulloch. It was here that Seaforth's
factor, Donald Murchison, successfully beat off
a party of Government troops in 1721.

would maintain the new road and allow the public over it, if the public used the new route and left the old, so that the lodge could be more private.

The old route, which is still a right-of-way and can therefore still be used, and which commands fine views of Mam Sodhail, went on the south side of the lochs. It leaves the modern route at the head of Glen Affric and goes by Athnamulloch to Loch Pollain Buidhe and Loch an Eang down to Tomich by the Knockfin Pass. Both the new and the old route, therefore, lead into Strath Glass.

Athnamulloch, the ford of the Mull men, was the scene of an exciting little skirmish in 1721. The estates of the Earl of Seaforth were forfeit after the '15 rising, but Seaforth's Factor, Donald Murchison, continued to collect the rents and send them to the Laird in France. In 1721, William Ross of Easter Fearn and his brother, Robert Ross, set off with a company of soldiers to try and stop Donald's illegal performances. Donald, however, got word of their coming, and lay in wait for them as they tried to make over to Kintail. There was an exchange of fire at Athnamulloch, in which William Ross was wounded together with a number of others, William's son being fatally wounded. The result was that the forces of the law had to retire home again leaving Donald Murchison to go on gathering rents to send to the exile. There is a monument to Murchison on the Loch Alsh shore of Kyle Akin.

In some other districts, not so readily guarded perhaps as Kintail, the people on the forfeited estates paid their rents twice over—once to the Government and once to the exiled Chief.

There is an amusing poem with an account of Donald Murchison's doings and also of the state of the roads at that time, which was published in 1737. It relates how

> Keppoch, Rob Roy, and Daniel Murchison,
> Cadets or servants to some Chief of clan;

From thefts or robbings scarce did ever cease,
Yet 'scaped the halter each and died in peace.
This last his exiled master's rents collected,
Nor unto King or law would be subjected;
Tho' veteran troops upon the confines lay,
Sufficient to make lord and tribe a prey.
Yet passes strong through which no roads were cut,
Safe guarded Seaforth's clan each in his hut;
Thus in stronghold the rogue securely lay,
Neither could they by force be driven away;
Till his attainted Lord and Chief of late
By ways and means repurchased his estate.

Now Beinn Fhada is a long ridge of a mountain, which extends from the head of Loch Duich to the head of Glen Affric, and it is therefore possible to walk upon either side of it from Kintail to the east. The right-of-way along the southern flank, through Gleann Lichd, is a well-marked path but is less impressive than that on the northern flank. The view of the Five Sisters from the path is good, but one is too close under them to realise their form and size properly.

The route branches off above Alltbeath and goes past the ruin of Camban, once the highest inhabited house in Rossshire. Below is the Allt Cam-ban—the white twisted stream (it has a sharp right-angle bend) and the glen is the Fionngleann —the white glen. Perhaps the snow lies there sooner than elsewhere. It is an easy climb from Affric up to Camban and over the watershed at 1,200 feet, but the way has some very steep sections as it pitches down into Glen Lichd. The burn, the Allt Granda, courses in a deep ravine cut in the schists and there are several waterfalls, of which one, a high lacy cascade is very fine. The name means the ugly precipice, the word *allt* having its old meaning of a height or precipice, not as in modern Gaelic, a stream.

From Kintail, the encirclement of Beinn Fhada (also called

Attow), makes a pleasant walk of 20 miles; and it is perhaps better to make this round and then explore the lower portion of Glen Affric separately, rather than march doggedly through from Kintail to Cannich.

The long straight glen of Strath Glass into which Glens Canich, Affric and Strathfarrar open, has been eroded along the line of a fault or breakage line in the schists. In the upper part, the broad valley is floored with a wide spread of alluvial deposits through which the river meanders; farther on, it escapes eastward through the deep ravines of the Druim Gorge, cut in Middle Old Red Sandstone conglomerates. Before these gorges were cut, it seems that the Strath Glass waters would be ponded back to form a long narrow lake like that of Ness. The gorges have been cut since the melting of the ice sheets.

Strath Glass is also of interest as an example of a valley which has captured the waters of one of the old consequent streams which originally flowed down Glen Cannich and through Glen Urquhart. The lower portion of the glen seems to have been once called Strath Farrar; Glen Strathfarrar meaning the glen portion of the broader strath which extended beyond its present nominal boundary at Struy. But the whole valley is now called Strath Glass and Strath Farrar is only known in the combination Glen Strathfarrar. According to this old naming, Strath Glass would be the portion from Tomich to Struy, and Strath Farrar the part from Struy to the Beauly Firth.

It was down this valley that the travellers, who had come over the hills from the west, went on to the east coast.

VII

THE ROAD BY THE SEA

CHAPTER XII

THE HILLS OF NO COMPROMISE

THESE are the hills of no compromise. These are the hills which guard the sanctuary of Applecross; the cruel, naked hills. They rise above Loch Kishorn in red walls of Torridon sandstone, massive guardians, Beinn Bhan, Sgurr a'Chaorachain, Meall Gorm.

Over them goes the Bealach na Ba, the Pass of the Cattle, claimed as the steepest motoring road in Britain, a six mile ascent with a general gradient of 1 in 8·2, rising to 1 in 5. The Bealach na Ba is the only road into Applecross, the little village that lies at the head of a wide, sandy bay on the triangular peninsula of Applecross between Loch Torridon and Loch Kishorn. The Bealach na Ba clambers up over the Torridon sandstone in three sharp hairpin bends and comes out on a red sandstone plateau at 2,053 feet, with a view out over the Isles and north and south along the mainland coast. Till May, the snow may block the only road to Applecross, and Applecross depends more on the sea for its supplies and mails than on the road.

Torridon sandstone is an ill rock for a Sasunnach to cross, far too much given to mural escarpments and overhanging cliffs to encourage familiarity. When I first saw the great hills of Applecross about the Bealach na Ba, I thought they were the most fearful hills in the whole world, and that no one could look upon them and live, like the head of Medusa. I was afraid, not of the steep road, but of the hills, when I drove over the Bealach; the way a little terrace on the rocky slope, with a long stretch of scree below, leading down to the white foaming burn.

But beyond these awful hills, lies the green plot of Apple-cross and the kirkyard where St. Maelrubha lies buried. And tradition has it that the man who gathers earth from the resting-place of Maelrubha may go to the ends of the earth and yet come safely back to Applecross.

There are other ways into Applecross that are open to the walker, and these ways run round by the coast, snuggled be-tween the sea and the red hills. The map shows a footpath leaving the Bealach na Ba road at Loch Kishorn, passing the keeper's house at Russel and going by the empty shells of Airidh-drishaig and Uags, round the headland of Rudha na h-Uamha to Toscaig. From Toscaig there is a road into Applecross.

It was a hot and sultry day that I followed this track to Applecross. Thunder seemed in the offing; banks of mist lay between the hills of Skye and the mainland in the deep hollow of Kyle of Lochalsh. The walls of red sandstone rose above Loch Kishorn in a veil of haze, which softened their outlines and coloured them a misty lilac. The sea in Loch Kishorn was clear and still, fringed by a brilliantly green flat of pasture land. At Courthill House, the vegetation seemed almost sub-tropical with red maples expanding their leaves, and bamboo mingling with primroses, violets and hart's tongue ferns. The tall beeches were in their first fresh flush of green; the bees were humming in the sycamore flowers.

The path down to Russel was distinct enough as it followed the shore. There are ruined houses at the stream mouth at Russel but a keeper still lives in an intact building, standing a little way back from the shore. The burn comes foaming down from a loch under the high crags of Sgurr a'Chaorachain (the Sheep Crag).

The keeper was walking outside his house when I came past. He said the path ahead was very faint, and that I, not knowing the route, would be more off the track than on it. But it never went more than 200 yards from the sea, and so that if one kept to the sea margin, there were no particular difficulties. "Then", said he, "there is a short cut over the hill tops from Airidh-drishaig to Toscaig, recently made and a good path." "Keep your eyes on the ground all the way", he went on, "it's the best place in the West Highlands for adders." He said he always liked to know where passers-by were heading for, "in case of anyone going amissing".

He was right about the track. It is nearly lost. Sometimes I had the trace of it and sometimes I did not. Sometimes I wandered off onto peat-cutting tracks and had to circle back to the sea. Sometimes I scrambled up and down little ledges of red sandstone. It was hard and rough going, and the miles went by very slowly.

Meall Gorm above me, had its lower slopes hung with birch and verdant green grass; and along the lower parts of all the hillsides were wide carpets of primroses, bluebells, marsh orchids, and sometimes bushes of gorse by the sea cliffs. The sea came into beautiful little bays or plashed round rocky little headlands, each inviting one to halt and go no farther. Oyster catchers rose from the shore, and shags stood motionless on jutting rocks. The red Torridon sandstone made all the beaches of a ruddy sand and shingle. The streams from the heights came down to the sea in cascades and pools.

But it was a very long way to Airidh-drishaig, where the empty house is still roofed and decent looking. Farther back, I had passed many old ruins and patches of once cultivated land. A boat from across Loch Kishorn was fishing off the coast, and I watched it, wondering where it was from. Eventually it started up its engine and went scudding off across the loch in the direction of Plockton.

The trail is perhaps one of the most lonely in Scotland. The boat was the only sign of living men that I saw all the way from Russel to Toscaig. Sheep were few and far between; two deer scuffled away up the hill from the shore as I passed them. It was a still pattern of hard red rocks and dulled sea, with threatening skies and a mist on the distant hills which continually made as if to roll over all the land.

I take it that it is possible to go round the headland by Uags, but at Airidh-drishaig I had had enough of picking an uncertain way over rock and bog, and turned up the rough but distinct track over the hills.

It is a hard track, with no more compromise about it than the red hills over which it leads. It climbs steeply, straight away up, with no attempt to make easy grades. The storms have torn down it and grubbed stones from it, and made many parts very rough. Streams are crossed on bridges.

It is a strange, wild world that the road to Toscaig takes, between masses of red and purple sandstone, past little tarns which lie black and still under the rocks, broken by the widening ripple rings as a fish rises. The land between the rocks is dark heathery moor, peaty and acid and sterile. And I walked alone over it, and came suddenly to the heights above Toscaig and looked down upon the sea and the island of Raasay and the pointed hills of Skye. And all the hills of the islands were hazy and blue in the heat, like outlines cut in flat boards.

Then, as the track pitches downwards again to Toscaig, there is a sudden view of the Toscaig river, flowing in a deep cleft in the red rocks, overhung by green trees, peat-stained, soft verdure in a barren country.

So, eventually the road is reached at the crofts of Toscaig, where they still work a sort of primitive strip cultivation of the land, and the arable ground is all dotted with piles of stone dug out of the soil. Crossing the Toscaig river by a bridge, one again looks up its cool, tree lined gorge with its red cliffs, and then strikes off along the coast to Applecross. As I traversed the last stretch by the sea, through the townships of Camasterach, Camusteel and Milton, boats riding at anchor in the inlets, and the high posts for the drying of nets by the houses, the tide was out and the scent of hot seaweed overwhelmed all the senses. It came in from the shore in great waves of hot air, intoxicating, maddening, like the road which stretched on and on and never seemed to come to Applecross.

CHAPTER XIII

THE SANCTUARY OF APPLECROSS

THE village of Applecross crouches on the seashore, clinging to a narrow strip of land between cliff and beach. It looks almost as if it were resisting being pushed off the land into the sea, which is sober fact, for this is the last foothold that the people held to when they were evicted from their holdings farther inland to make place for deer.

> Woe be to them who choose for a clan
> Four-footed people.

Applecross bay has a pleasant air of greenness. All around are the red hills, but here, at the mouth of the Applecross river, are green fields and woods and a profusion of ferns, mare's and horse tails under the trees, with bright plots of primroses and scented banks of gorse. The tide runs out to expose wide stretches of red sand derived from the red hills; the sea is so clear that standing on the hill above you can look down through the green depths to the waving forests of seaweed. Out over the sea are the islands of Raasay and Skye, sometimes very close and clear to see, sometimes fading into a mysterious haze like isles in some lost story of a forgotten land. Out, circling over the bright sea, are the gannets, dropping in sudden swoops into the water for fish, striking the water a tremendous smack and disappearing in spurts of spray. The fish caught and eaten, they are off and up again, circling and diving.

The Broch of Dun Telve, Gleann Beag, Glen Elg

Ruaridh Mor MacAogan's Cross, Applecross

Along the foreshore of Applecross toward the next hamlet of Milton, a grey limestone forms a natural breakwater. The limestone is of Liassic age, and has been worked for local use in the past. Across the bay, the Torridon sandstone, against which the very much younger Liassic beds are faulted, forms steep red cliffs. On the red sandstone grows grey and yellow lichen, and in the cracks of the rock, thrift.

Applecross in Gaelic is A'Comaraich (the Sanctuary) for here in ancient times was a famous place of refuge. Applecross' name is always linked with that of Maelrubha and the little church that he founded at the mouth of the river. Beside the shell of the little pre-Reformation chapel, under a low mound of earth, Maelrubha is buried; Maelrubha who seems nearly always to be confused with other people and other rites.

Applecross itself is a corruption of the name Apor-crossan —the mouth of the Crossan river. The tradition is that a proprietor did not like the sound of Apor-crossan and made the change deliberately, planting five apple trees cross-wise in his garden to commemorate the alteration. But Apor-crossan could easily change in ordinary use into the more easily said Applecross. Another story relates the name to the fact that an apple tree in the monk's garden bore fruit marked with a cross!

Maelrubha's name means the servant or boy of the headland. St. Columba is the only saint of the Irish-Scottish Celtic Church to take precedence over St. Maelrubha. Maelrubha was born on A.D. 3rd January 642 in Ireland. His father was Elganach, and on his father's side, Maelrubha was eighth in descent from Niall of the Nine Hostages. His mother was called Subtan or Suaibsech, and was the sister of St. Comgall, Abbot of Bangor, and of the race of the Irish Picts—the Fiacha Araidhe. There seems to be a difficulty in supposing that Subtan was the sister of Comgall, for Comgall died at a great age in A.D. 602.

Following the custom in the Celtic Church of more or less family associations of monks, Maelrubha became a member of Comgall's abbey at Bangor. In 671, when he was 29, he crossed over to Scotland, and in 673 founded a church at Applecross. He lived at Applecross for 51 years, making various missionary journeys through the country from this centre, and died there in 722, on Tuesday 21st April, at the age of 80 years 3 months and 19 days.

He is commemorated in many churches in Scotland, a great number of which, including that on Isle Maree, he must have founded himself. In the Celtic Church, the various churches were called after their founders. The name of Loch Maree is derived from that of Maelrubha, and his name appears in a great number of place names. In Harris, one swears by him, exclaiming "Ma-Ruibhe!"

Maelrubha's day is 21st April, but the Scottish Church does not observe this date but 27th August. It appears that Maelrubha has been confused with St. Rufus of Capua, and that the day was changed accordingly. St. Maelrubha's fair (the Feil Maree), which was discontinued in 1880, was held in Contin on the last Wednesday in August.

Maelrubha is often said to have been killed by the Norse in Easter Ross. But the Norsemen did not begin their invasions until after Maelrubha was dead, and it seems that here again there has been confusion with some other person. Maelrubha was succeeded at Applecross by Failbhe, who was drowned at sea, and who was followed by Ruaridh Mor MacAogan. Ruaridh Mor did encounter the Vikings, for they ravaged Applecross sometimes between 790 and 800, and Ruaridh had to escape to the parent monastery in Bangor. Ruaridh became Abbot there, but was brought back to Applecross for burial. The body is said to have come floating on the waves on a flat stone. The stone was erected at the head of the grave and stood the same height as Ruaridh.

About 150 years ago, the stone was moved to its present position by the churchyard door. It is of local Torridon sand-stone, 9 feet high, 2 feet 10 inches broad, and 3 inches thick, and has a collared Celtic cross carved on its face.

But perhaps the most interesting part of the history of Maelrubha is that of how his memory became fused with older pagan rights, and the Christian saint became a sort of god to Applecross and Loch Maree. The well on Isle Maree was supposed to cure insanity, and coins were stuck into a sacred tree as an offering to the resident spirits. Queen Victoria visited the island and added a coin.

Lunatics were made to drink water from the well and were towed three times round the island. The well is supposed to have lost its power after a sceptical shepherd dipped a mad dog in it. In 1858, the treatment was applied to a mad woman, who became a raging maniac after it; in 1868, the same treat-ment cured a male lunatic.

On the island too, bulls were sacrificed to Maelrubha. On the 6th August 1678, the minister of Gairloch reported to Dingwall Presbytery that he had "sumonded by his officer to this prebrie day, Hector MacKenzie in Mellan, in the Parish of Gerloch, as also John, Murdoch and Duncan McKenzies, sons to the said Hector, also Kenneth McKenneth, his grandson, for sacrificing a bull in ane heathnish manner in the iland of St. Ruffus, commonlie called Ellan Moury in Lochew for the recovering of the health of Cirstane MacKenzie, spouse to the said Hector MacKenzie, who was formerlie sick and vale-tudinarie".

The rites connected with Maelrubha were a concern of the Presbytery for many years, and appear to have persisted in spite of their efforts, for measures were taken against them in 1656, and the sacrifice for the benefit of Cirstane MacKenzie was made in 1678.

On the 5th September 1656, Dingwall Presbytery met at

I

Applecross, and the records of their meeting give a fairly detailed account of the Applecross rites:

The said day the Pbrie of Dingwall, according to the appoyntment of Synode for searcheing and censureing such principalls and superstitious practizes as sould be discovered thaire, haveing mett at Appilcross, and finding amongst wᵞʳ abominable and heathinishe practizes that the people in that place were accustomed to sacrifice bulls at a certaine tyme wppon the 25 of August, wᶜ day is dedicate as they conceave to St. Mourie, as they call him, and that thair wer frequent approaches to some ruinous chappells and circulateing of them, and that future events in reference especiallie to lyf and death in taking of jurneys was expect to be manifested by a holl of a round stone. qrein they tryed the entreing of thair heade, wᶜ if could doe, to witt, be able to put in thaire heade, they expect thair returneing to that place, and faileing, they conceaved it ominous; and withall thair adoreing of wells, and wther superstitious monuments and stones tedious to rehearse, have appoynted as followes: That quhosoever sall be found to commit such abhominationes, especaillie sacrifices of ony kind or at ony tyme, sall publickly appeire and be rebuked in sackcloath sex severall lords dayis in sex several churches, viz. Lochcarron, Appilcross, Contane, Fottertie, Dingwell, and last in Garloch paroch church, and that they may wppon the delatione of the sessioune and minister of that paroche he sall cause sumond the guiltie persoune to compeire befoire the Pbrie to be convinced, rebuked and yreto be injoyned his censore, and with all that the Justice sould be acquent to doe yʳᵉ deuties in suppressing of the forsaid wickedness, and the forsaid censure in reference to thaire sacrificeing to be made vse of incace of convict and appeireing and evidences of remors be found: and, faileing, that they be censureing wt excomumicaone.

Dingwall Presbytery went on from Applecross to Kinlochewe, where they met on the 9th September and heard more details of the worship of Mourie, including the "poureing of milk wpon hills as ablaones". The parishes of Lochcarron, Lochalsh, Kintail, Contin, Foddertie and Lochbroom were said to be the worst offenders.

The various stones in the ruin of the old chapel at Applecross were destroyed to stop their superstitious use. It is also
said that there were many interesting monuments in the graveyard, which originally stretched from the shore to the hillside.
These last were removed, when the churchyard was reduced
in size to make more room for the minister's glebe.

There were also stones marking the six mile limits of the
sanctuary area, but these too are all gone. The last was smashed
by a mason when a school was being built nearby, about 80
years ago. There was only one other great area of sanctuary
in the north, that of St. Duthac at Tain. This was also marked
out by stones, and the boundaries are more exactly known
than that of Applecross.

Applecross had, according to the old *Statistical Account*
written in 1792, an earth house, which was faced with stones
inside and roofed with flags overlain with turves. It also had
a "Danish Dun" or broch. In those days, the parish kept
about 3,000 black cattle, so there is small wonder that the pass
over the hills is called the pass of the cattle! The cattle
were "coupled"—one calf being reared by two cows.

In 1792, every man was both a farmer and a fisher, built
his own house and made his own shoes. The hand quern was
still in regular use, because the mill was badly situated and
troublesome to take the grain to. The local smiths were paid
in meal and had a right to the head of every cow slaughtered in
the parish. The rate of exchange for meal was a peck to the
half merk Scots.

This right of the smiths to the head of any slaughtered cattle
in the parish seems to be linked with the bull sacrifices to
Maelrubha. The bull was killed by the smith, who took the
head in payment. This, I believe, is according to the custom
of the Druids.

There still seems to linger a sense of quiet and peace over
the glen where Maelrubha is buried. Men say that no one can

injure themselves or commit suicide in sight of it. I narrowly escaped treading on an adder there, which might be interpreted either way. Even in the sanctuary of Applecross the old proverb is still true: *Am fear a sheallas roimhe cha tuislich e* (He who looks before him will not stumble).

CHAPTER XIV

THE ROAD TO LOCH MAREE

WHEN St. Maelrubha went from Applecross to his
church on Isle Maree, he went up the broad open
valley of the Applecross river, and crossed over the
hills at a height of 1,213 feet to Shieldaig on Loch Torridon.
Thence he must have followed the coast round to the head of
Loch Torridon and gone up Glen Torridon, past Loch Clair
and down to Kinlochewe.

The direct crossing to Shieldaig is short and easy along the
old track, but there is a longer route going round the coast.
This is a well-kept path, about five feet wide, which follows
the edge of the Applecross peninsula round by Rudha na Fearn
and along the shore of Loch Torridon. From Applecross to
Shieldaig by this path is about 25 miles. It serves a number of
small hamlets along the shore, and must closely resemble the
original state of the path from Russel by Uags to Toscaig, when
the ruins along that way were inhabited.

When I left Applecross to follow the path by the sea, it
was raining hard, but a small patch of blue sky gave a promise
of better things to come. The rain came down heavily, pat-
tering on the broad leaves of the sycamores, and the hills of
Skye and Raasay were dim and blue.

The peninsula round which the way goes is mostly carved
in Torridon sandstone, but there it forms much lower land
than to the southward, and inland is mostly a broad and undulating peat moor with scattered crops of red rock. The

road climbs steeply up the hillside from Applecross kirk, to round the headland of Rudha na Guailne, and the view is back over the bay to the white houses of Applecross and the green trees at the mouth of the Applecross river. Rainbows came and went as the sun broke through the clouds, and storms chased each other out over the Atlantic to the Isles.

The long island of Raasay lies between the mainland and Skye, with green terraced hills. Beyond rises the Storr (2,360 ft.) in Skye. The sun came glinting on to the Storr, bringing every detail into clear relief, whilst Raasay stood out in black relief. Next to Raasay and to the northward, lies the island of Rona, a low, darker island than Raasay, rounded in its hills and carved of the Lewisian gneiss. A lighthouse showed white on Rona. As the rain came over the two islands, with the sun behind them, the narrow Caol Rona between them was spanned by a rainbow, whose red band was a flaming orange fire of light.

It was of Rona that Sir Donald Munro wrote in 1549, that it was "full of wood and heddir, with ane havin for heiland galeys in the middis of it, and the same havein is guyed for fostering of theives, ruggairs, and reivairs, till a nail, upon the peilling and spulzeing of poure pepill. This ile perteins to M'Gillychallan of Raarsay by force, and to the bishope of the iles be heritage."

The track comes down to the bay of Sand in a couple of hairpin bends and a 1 in 4 gradient. Sand is the sort of beach that in Cornwall or Devon would be overrun by tourists. Here in the West Highlands, it is mournfully desolate. Between red sandstone cliffs, there lies a long and narrow bay, where the sea laps upon a wide spread of white sand. Beyond the sea rise the mysterious hills of Skye. At the head of the sandy beach is a green pasture leading up into a valley cut through the red sandstone, where tumbled blocks make caves and fantastic faces. And nobody lives at Sand now. There are the marks of cultivation on the green flat by the sea, and the ruins of houses, but Sand is deserted.

There is a house farther on down the road at Salacher, and a half-deserted hamlet farther on, called Lonbain. Once the sea stood at a higher level than it does now, and the old beach, now raised well above the waves, appears along the coast here as a green strip between blue sea and red cliffs and the brown inland moor. Everywhere that there is a bit of raised beach there have been houses and fields, but ruin is now everywhere evident.

Lonbain and Kalnakill sit on a long sweep of raised beach. There are still inhabited houses, but the rushes are creeping in over the fields, and there are holes in the roofs of many of the houses.

There was a little stir going on along the road. Surveyors' poles stood at intervals along the track. For this track has been surveyed with a view to the possibility of turning it into a good road into Applecross. If that comes about, I wondered, leaving the surveyors behind, will it come in time to save the villages? Or will it be like the Caledonian Canal, built to stop de-population and making an easy way out of the country? For roads alone will take people away, not keep them at home. As Ross-shire County have pointed out, any plan for the High-lands must be a co-ordinated scheme, bringing work and amenity as well as good transport.

Until I saw a tree growing outside a house, I had hardly realised that I was in a country without trees. Here there were none at all, bar this straggly pine. The old saying, *Tha mi na's eolaiche air coille na bhi fo eagal na cailleach-oidhche* (I am more accustomed to a wood than to be afraid of an owl) began to make sense.

The streams came down off the moorland in rough and rocky courses. The sea echoed in a dull roar from the caves along the cliffs. The sky was clearing, the sea lay like watered silk, the islands became clearer. I rounded a rise in the moor and suddenly saw the great masses of the hills of Torridon sandstone about Upper Loch Torridon. The sea between them and the peninsula on which I walked was out of sight and they seemed to spring from the brown moor itself.

Cuaig is a small hamlet quite hid in the folds of the moor, and clustered beside a little burn. It is suddenly seen as one enters it, and equally suddenly lost to sight as one leaves it. A small terrier came yapping at my heels; there was a red letter box set in a wall. Farther down the road was the town peat cutting, and a man came out of a house and came after me to fetch peats, carrying a peat creel (Gaelic *Cliabh Moine*) to bring them back in. Peat reek filled all the air about these hamlets, and each had extensive cuttings. Cutting was taking place when I passed by, the surface turf being removed with the long-handled *cabar lar* (turf parer) and then the soft peat cut into neat blocks and laid out to dry with the *tor-sgian* (peat knife). Later, when it has hardened, it is set up into small heaps of four or five peats in a kind of pyramid. After further drying and hardening, it is put into bigger piles and eventually carried home.

Fearnmore, the hamlet by Rudha na Fearn, the point of the peninsula which forms the south side of Loch Torridon, was heralded by a herd of black and red cattle, browsing by the roadside. The road twisted between reedy little lochs and then ran through the hamlet. I looked back to Skye and Raasay. When I had rounded the point they would be out of sight. The weather had cleared and it was brilliantly sunny and very hot. Out to sea, I could see the outline of Lewis. Up the sea loch Torridon, there was a tremendous prospect of mountains —Beinn Alligin, Liathach and the rest; the quartzite peaks of the Coulins glinting in the bright light. This view continues in sight all the way to Shieldaig, but with infinite variations, as the hills become closer at hand.

The outbuildings at places like Fearnmore are built in dry

stone of Torridon sandstone boulders. The rocks are just as
they have been collected and are in no way shaped. The roofs
are thatched with fern and heather.

At Fearnmore, I saw a woman carrying a full peat-creel to
the house. There is no other means of transport. The road is
too narrow for a cart, and so there are no horses. The post,
—every hamlet has a letter box—is collected by sea. Motor
cycles can be used on the narrow path, and they are the only
means of rapid movement.

I walked on beside Loch Torridon, and eventually just
beyond Arinacrinachd, came to a wood. It was a very low
wood of birches, hazel and rowan. But the stunted trees were
very old with immensely thick and gnarled trunks. Arinacrinachd is quite a large place, boasting a school and a post office.

The Lewisian gneiss outcrops along the coast a little farther
on, and also forms a great bare rounded mass of rock across
the loch at Diabaig. The next hamlet is Kenmore, where a
boat was anchored out in the bay, and a path returns over the
moor to Applecross. Farther on, I came into another wood,
that was full of primroses, and a narrow little bay, red cliffed,
with deep, green water and the skeleton of a boat on the beach.
Above the bay was a ruined house built of red sandstone, and
a garden gone to waste, with a big clump of rhubarb. Beside
it, a brown peat-stained burn came tumbling down from lochs
far away up on the moors.

The track began to climb up to the heights of the hill called
A'Bhaintir (572 ft.), from the top of which one looks down
upon the bay of Loch Torridon called Loch Shieldaig and over
the shining water to the Torridon mountains. Shieldaig lies
just across the bay, but it is a long, long way yet to walk.
First, there is a very steep descent down the hill again to the
village of Ardheslaig. Then, the way undulates up and down,
up and down, almost endlessly. Stunted pines begin to appear,
growing larger as one goes on; attractive islets lie near the

shore; there are several fine burns which cascade down to the
sea. The heat became over-powering and the scent of the pines
filled all the air. When at last, I came into the long straggly
village of Shieldaig, all I desired was to get out of the blinding
sunlight into somewhere dark.

Onward from Shieldaig, the right-of-way runs beside Loch
Torridon to join the highroad at the head of the loch. It runs
between the high mural precipices of Torridon sandstone which
form the hills of Ben-Damph forest, and the clear green-blue
water of upper Loch Torridon. From Annat, where the road
is joined, a right-of-way runs over the Bealach na Lice to
Strath Carron. The path looks a most interesting one to travel,
but I have never been over it. The name Annat means the
relic chapel of a saint and is found in a number of places in
Scotland.

The last ten miles up Glen Torridon on the line of St.
Maelrubha's route to Isle Maree are on a hard white road,
which the hot sun can make almost blinding. The road is
worth walking for the views that one can get of the great face
of the mountain Liathach. The ridge of this mountain—the
name means the Grey One—is five miles long, and it rises
almost sheerly, bare Torridon sandstone, from the road to
3,456 feet. The walker can go slowly along for the five miles,
stopping frequently to look up the great crags and pinnacles
and see how the form of the mountain develops as he passes
along onward. He will almost certainly soon begin to plan the
ascent, for Liathach is a hill of challenge. But let no one go
lightly upon the crags of Liathach, for there can be no compromise with the cruel red Torridon sandstone.

Where one crosses the watershed and begins to go downhill
toward Kinlochewe, is a Suidhe or resting-place of St. Maelrubha. Much later, somewhere between 1727 and 1731,
another minister rested there. He was the Reverend Mr. Sage
who had the difficult task of ministering to the rather wild

inhabitants. He was going back to Gairloch one day, accompanied only by a lad who carried the lunch done up in a cloth. Two parishioners overtook them, and when the minister sat down for his lunch, at the crossing of the Allt a'Choire Dhiubh Mhoir (the burn of the large black corry), these two sat one on either side of him. They then announced that they were going to murder him. Mr. Sage, however, was a powerful man and he acted quickly. He seized each assailant round the neck and more or less knocked their heads together until such time as they abandoned their project!

Aeneas Sage was involved in another fight at Toscaig. At Toscaig, one Calum Ruadh lived with two women, his lawful wife and one Mairearad Nighinn Dhomhnuill Dhuinn Mhic Rath, both of whom bore him children. Calum was duly cited by the Session, but took no notice, and Mr. Sage decided to pay a visit to Toscaig. In answer to his knock at the door, Calum appeared with his dirk drawn. In a flash, the minister had his own knife out, and the battle began. Calum was overpowered and Mr. Sage imposed his own terms.

Across the glen from the crossing of the Allt a'Choire Dhuibh Mhoir, is Lochan an Iasgaich and above it, Coire Cheud Cnoc—the corry of a hundred hillocks. These innumerable little hillocks represent the terminal moraines of one of the local glaciers during the waning phases of the glacial period.

The way goes on past Loch Bharranch and Loch Clair and past some fine native pines, down to Cromasag, where I startled some red deer, and to Kinlochewe. There, perhaps, Maelrubha embarked for Isle Maree. There, certainly, the walker from the sanctuary of Applecross will know that Applecross will draw him back again, over the red sandstone hills.

THE ROAD ACROSS THE NORTH OF SCOTLAND

CHAPTER XV

ULLAPOOL TO OYKELL BRIDGE

EAST to west, Scotland at her narrowest is only 26 miles across—from the head of the Dornoch Firth to Loch Broom on the West Coast. It is almost on the line of this narrow waist that the track from Ullapool to Oykell Bridge crosses the north of Scotland, following a through valley, and climbing only 850 feet, to cross the watershed of Drum Albyn.

Ullapool itself is a trim little township of white-washed houses, placed upon a green flat beside the clear waters of Loch Broom, the brown hills rising behind it. The streets cross each other at right angles; there are broad grass verges between house front and road, for Ullapool was laid out as a model village. That was in 1788, when the British Fisheries Society had hopes of making Ullapool the chief centre for the West Coast fishings. Earlier, Inverlael, at the head of Loch Broom, had been the principal village of the district. But the name of Ullapool is Norse, and records that here was the farm of some forgotten Viking named Ulli.

Out to sea are the Summer Isles, where the fiord of Loch Broom widens out into the Atlantic; islands wonderfully attractive as one watches the sun sink into the sea beyond them, the western sky patterned with gold and pink. Tanera, Dr. Fraser Darling's farming experiments have made famous; earlier, like Ullapool, it had a fishing station. There was another fishing station on Isle Martin, started by a London company and a Mr.

Moriston of Stornoway in 1785; their operations ended soon after Moriston's death in 1791. The fish from these stations were exported to Leith, Greenock and Ireland. Ullapool's red-herring house produced 500 barrels in 1794.

Isle Martin is close to the mainland. On it, a stone with an inscribed cross is said to mark the grave of a priest who had earlier lived on Priest Island, far out to sea at the mouth of Loch Broom. The story goes that the bishop of the diocese banished the priest to the island, and that he lived in various caves, shifting from one to the other according to the weather, and later venturing back nearer the mainland to Isle Martin.

In March, I found it was already spring in Ullapool. The snowdrops were fading, and in the fertile gardens along Loch Broom-side, there were bright patches of blue and yellow crocus, golden daffodils and paler primroses, the red of the flowering currant, the sticky horse chestnut buds unfolding. In the village the tall palms outside the houses seemed to match ill with the line of the brown hills with the snow-wreaths still in their corries. Then, in the evening, the moon was suddenly hidden by racing, ragged cloud, and hail fell inch deep round the palms, burying the primroses. Even in sheltered Ullapool, March in Scotland had a sting in its tail.

The present main road to Ullapool from the south leaves the Dingwall-Achnasheen road at Garve, and follows a barren and deserted cross-country valley to the head of Loch Broom. Before it descends to Loch Broom it passes close above the gorge of Corrieshalloch, the waters of which flow into Loch Broom. Of all Scottish ravines, Corrieshalloch is perhaps the most dramatic. One descends from the bleak and peaty uplands; in front is a glimpse of the green fertility of Loch Broom-side, and unexpectedly close is the wound of Corrieshalloch. The road keeps to a narrow terrace above the gorge; below the rock walls are clean cut and almost vertical, a narrow trench cut downwards 200 feet.

The Abhainn Droma (called the river Broom below the gorge) plunges through the gorge in waterfalls, of which the Measach fall is said to be 270 feet high. On moonlit nights, a ghostly stag pursued by a ghostly hound, are supposed to leap the falls. In life, they are said to have attempted the jump and fallen into the river. Whoever sees the ghostly stag leap across, sees his own reflection in its eyes.

Below Corrieshalloch, at Inverbroom, in 1896, a keeper found a bronze sword in a cleft of rock on the hillside. There is no story to the find, but that the sword was a rare type, in which blade, hilt and pommel were all cast in metal, and that it appears to date from the late Bronze Age. And yet one cannot but wonder about its original owner and how it came to lie in a cleft of rock above Loch Broom. Was he of the sword perhaps killed there, or did he lose it by accident, or drop it or hide it?

The gorge of Corrieshalloch seemed to set the pattern for all the rivers and burns that I passed on the way from Ullapool to Oykell Bridge. The rocks through which they were cut were various, but the trench-like pattern was the same—the narrow cleft with sheer walls, the plunging water.

I left Ullapool for Oykell Bridge on a cold March morning. The sun was out and the sky clear, though little pink clouds at sunrise forecast no particular good. The Oykell Bridge track turns off about half a mile out of Ullapool at the bridge over the Ullapool river which carries the main road northward to Assynt. The river runs trenched in red Torridon sandstone, the rock hung with gorse and birch. The track turned up beside the river, keeping fairly near to it, and wandering in a leisurely fashion over brown moorlands. It is a good shooting lodge track, maintained as such as far as Rhidorroch Old Lodge some seven miles up the glen.

Behind there was a glimpse of the Summer Isles, and across Loch Broom the square heathery mountain of Beinn Ghobhlach

K

("The Forked Mountain"), 2,082 feet, the outcrops of rock near his summit picked out in freshly fallen snow. Farther back, between Beinn Ghobhlach and Beinn nam Ban, the rocky upsweep of the Sail Mhor ("The Big Heel"), 2,508 feet, of Dundonnell rose, glittering with snow, a massive pile of Torridon sandstone.

These mountains, Sail Mhor and Beinn Ghobhlach, remained long in sight as I walked on up the glen of the Ullapool river. In coming the other way, from Oykell Bridge, I considered how one would sight them and suppose that the journey was nearing the end, when there were still some six miles or so yet to walk. And in fact, long distance views of the way ahead are a feature of the whole route; a tiring feature, for to see mile after mile of the track undulating in front of one makes the way seem longer than it is. It is corners that make a road seem short to walk.

The red rock soon gave place to the grey silver colouring of the Cambrian quartzites; a line of grey crags set in bright green turf which snaked across the brown moors, marked an outcrop of Cambrian limestone. It had been quarried at one or two small openings beside the track. In front, grey Moine schists rose in craggy cliffs beyond Loch Achall.

Loch Achall, from which the Ullapool river flows, is a loch of few features, a small lake amongst rolling, heather-covered hills, scrubby birch woods on its shore. The wind brought the water up in little ripples on the shingle beach, and the sun gave it that deep blue which always seems to come to peaty water. Later in the year, when the woods are green and the heather flowering, Loch Achall is probably quite different to look at; in the middle of March it is almost unrelievedly bare and bleak.

Rhidorroch Lodge is snugly placed beside the loch, hidden amongst plantations of fir and trimmed beech hedges. The best portion of the road ends at this lodge; the section beyond it leading to Rhidorroch Old Lodge is narrower and of poorer surface.

The track goes on up the valley, a glen level-floored, with steep hillsides edged with crags, down which streams cascade. The most dramatic is the Eas a'Chraosain burn. The Eas is a great cleft through the schist heights; its east wall apparently vertical, the western one somewhat inclined. The burn flows in a white ribbon on the floor of this cut in the rock, a tiny rivulet dwarfed by tremendous cliffs.

Above Loch Achall, the river is the Rhidorroch. It meanders through the marshy flats and flows under the high crag faces of Creags Ghrianach and Ruadh. These cliffs rise sheerly from the valley floor, their faces trenched by storms, a litter of fallen rock at their feet. The wind growled against them, and I looked back to dark clouds piling up in the western sky, and wondered whether I could beat the bad weather to Oykell Bridge.

Glen Achall itself, as I went on up it, had pleasant natural woods. There were a few stray pines on the rocks of Creag Ghrianach, and across the river, a whole wood of them. Beside the track, were alders and birches, the birch twigs vivid crimson with the rising sap.

At Rhidorroch Old Lodge the good track ends. The right-of-way goes straight on, a distinct path but with some very wet portions. The Lodge itself is across the river and reached by a footbridge.

The Allt an Luchda joins the Rhidorroch near the lodge and its lower course is all set with shapely native pines. So, too, is the course of the Rhidorroch itself, running well below the line now taken by the track. Just before the main east-west watershed is reached, the river turns in a right-angle bend to the south into Glen Douchary, and from the track, one can look up this glen and see the water foaming over great waterfalls and cascades, beside which yet more pines grow.

The track climbs steeply up to the watershed ridge. In front, the long narrow Loch an Daimh (the Loch of the Stag), was for a few moments blue, till the threatening storms clouded the sky. I looked back down Glen Achall toward Ullapool. The wind came rushing up the glen from the west and the sky gave promise of snow. I saw the serrate tops of An Teallach with the snow thick upon them and I saw them haze over with a veil of sleet. Southward the same haze fell about the crag of Creag an Duine. There was a spit of cold rain in the wind now: I hastened down the path in the hope that in crossing the watershed I would leave the main storm behind me in the high mountains of the west.

Creag an Duine, of which I got tantalising glimpses from the track, must be one of the most attractive mountains in all Scotland. I saw its narrow ridge, with the little rocky turret at the tip, snow speckled, the rock showing through in dark lines, and the crag face plunging vertically down. It forms part of the great northern cliffs of Seana Bhraigh (the Old Brae), cliffs which drop 1,500 feet down to corrie lochs, and whose crests provide a high level walk at well over 3,000 feet.

The track keeps to the dryer ground well above the shore of Loch an Daimh. It is joined by another right-of-way which comes down Glen Douchary from Inverlael. This second route involves much more climbing than does the Ullapool route across Scotland, ascending 1,700 feet before descending into Glen Douchary. Roy's map of 1755 marks it as the road from Loch Broom to Tain.

The house of Knockdaimh beside the loch was deserted and long empty. Ahead the track grew wetter as it advanced toward the undulating uplands which edge Strath Oykell and Glen Einig. A string of deer appeared on the hill above, suitably Cnoc an Daimh (the Stag's Mount). They stood in a close row on the skyline watching me. I remembered a ghillie's statement: "If you are on a right-of-way and keeping going steadily on, the deer will realise that you are not hunting them and will not run away." I walked on and the deer remained where they were!

The burn from Loch an Daimh, the Abhainn Poiblidh, joins the Rappach Water some two miles below Knockdamph. The combined water is then the Einig, and some five miles farther down the glen it flows into the Oykell immediately below Oykell Bridge. There is a route up the Rappach Water to the west to Strath Kanaird eight miles north of Ullapool.

There are two alternative routes to Oykell Bridge from this point. One fords the Abhainn Poiblidh immediately above its junction with the Rappach. It is a good ford with a pebbly bottom but the current is swift and might give trouble in time of spate. The track continues along the south bank of the Einig, becoming a good shooting-lodge road at Duag bridge a mile and a half farther on.

The other route fords the Rappach and follows the north bank of the Einig and is only a path. The Rappach is a much more considerable river to ford than the Poiblidh, but before the construction of the bridge over the Duag, the northern route would probably have been the easier.

I crossed the Abhainn Poiblidh and took the southern route. The Einig entered another trenched ravine, grown with birch trees. The track kept to the higher and dryer ground till it joined the good track at Duag. The Duag is a dark and peaty stream which drops into the Einig in a fine series of waterfalls and plunge pools. At the bridge, there seemed no place where a ford was possible, unless like the Measach stag, one sprang across the rocks where they narrowed above a waterfall. The shooting lodge track, incidentally, turns up beside the Duag and goes to Corriemulzie Lodge and Loch a'Choire Mhoir under Seana Bhraigh.

The road at Oykell bridge, with cars passing along it, comes into sight soon after Duag bridge. The track undulates toward it, crossing all its streams, including the Einig close to Oykell Bridge, by bridges. Across the glen, it is possible to pick out the line of the northern path. There is also another track, which branches off from the track and goes southward into Srath Cuilionach to join the road down Strath Carron to Bonar Bridge. The start of this track appeared to be very indistinct and boggy.

So I came down to Strath Oykell and Amat, a farm in the crook of land between Einig and Oykell. Strath Oykell itself is one of the most important through valleys across the north of Scotland, leading through the hills from Bonar Bridge on the Dornoch Firth to Assynt in the West. It was this way that Lord Louden and President Forbes of Culloden retreated in 1746. After Lord Louden's attempt to surprise Prince Charles at Moy had ended in the Rout of Moy, the Government forces retreated northward. Louden supposed that all the Highland army was at Moy and hurried north intending to hold a line based on the river Shin. President Forbes went with him.

On 20th March, Charles' men took Dornoch in a surprise attack, and Louden, Forbes and some 800 men had to retreat cross-country to Skye. They went up Strath Oykell where they were on the 21st. On the 22nd they took the Oykell Bridge-Ullapool track and arrived at Loch Broom in the evening. Next day, they went on to Loch Maree by a track which runs from Braemore at the head of Corrieshalloch cross country to Kinlochewe via the Heights of Kinlochewe and Loch an Nid. From thence, they crossed the Coulin Pass into Strath Carron and eventually reached Skye on the 26th, where they are reported to have arrived in want of money, ammunition and provisions.

As I descended to Oykell Bridge, I looked westward over the moors to where the Assynt hills rose in fantastic shapes against the sky, a stormy sky of deep blue cloud and sweeping rain. I could look back along the track and see that higher up the glen it was already raining.

Northward, rose the great mass of Ben More Assynt (3,273 ft.) the highest point in Sutherland. It is mostly carved out of the Lewisian gneiss and is claimed as the oldest mountain over 3,000 feet in the country. Southward of Ben More was the rounded hump of Canisp; the two pillars of Suilven and the twin peaks of Cul Mhor, like dragon's teeth, rearing to the stormy sky. These three are remnants of Torridon sandstone, weathered relics of a once extensive mass of rock covering the undulating Lewisian gneiss from which they rise so strangely and suddenly.

No one seems to know the meaning of the name Oykell. The tidal part of the river was the boundary between the ancient province of Cat with Ross. Cat comprised modern Sutherland and Caithness and was divided into three parts: Ness (Caithness), Strathnaver (Northern Sutherland) and Sudrland (Sutherland south of Strathnaver).

The Norsemen called the Oykell, *Ekkjal* and the hills above it, *Ekkjals-bakki*—Oykell bank. The name may mean High Bank and be correlated with the "Ripa Alta" mentioned by Ptolemy. But there is no certainty of the meaning.

Two bridges now cross the Oykell at Oykell Bridge. The old one marks the county boundary between Ross and Sutherland; the new one, a little farther downstream, was made when the road was reconstructed, in recent years.

Outside the little inn beside the bridges is a monolith of schist over ten feet high. It looks ancient and bears Scandinavian runes. It was, in fact, pulled out of the river with the aid of many men, horses and a considerable amount of whisky, by a bored English angler in a bad fishing spell. This was done some 70 years ago. It was then devoid of runes.

Sometime later, a party of four on a walking tour, one of

whom could write runic, amused themselves by carving their names on the stone. Thus:

I   C   A   M   B   E   L   L

IX

THE FAR NORTH

CHAPTER XVI

MY LADY OF THE LITTLE LOCHS

THERE was a little cloud of spume over the headland across the bay, and the waves came in, out of a lavender sea to break in white and emerald and blue on the broad stretch of white sand. They came in with a deep-throated, hollow-sounding roar, and until I stepped down, off the sand dunes, and crossed the sand to the very edge of the Atlantic, I did not realise how rough the sea was. From the sand dunes, the waves looked almost ripple-sized; for Sandwood Bay is larger than at first appears.

Sandwood. I could see the lighthouse on Cape Wrath, half-a-dozen miles to the north. There was a mine washed up on the shingle bar between the beach and Sandwood loch, and a great hollow, littered with rusting splinters of metal, in the dunes, where some other mine maybe had exploded. And I had come past the masts of a disused radio station to this lonely bay, whose name harks back to earlier wars and the Norse invasion of the Scottish mainland.

In Sutherland, nearly half the place names along the coast are Norse, and there are even more in Caithness. Cape Wrath is derived from a Norse word for a turning point; and Sandwood is Sand-vatn—Sand water. The crofting township, near where I had left my car to walk across to Sandwood, is corrupted into Oldshore Beg; once it was Asleifarvik, and off it King Haco of Norway is said to have anchored his fleet in 1263. The exact date was the 10th of August. The fleet sailed on to the famous battle of Largs, which ended the Norse domination of the north of Scotland and the Hebrides. At Largs the Norse fleet was defeated, and three years later, at Perth, the Western Highlands and Islands were ceded to Scotland for a payment of 4,000 marks down, and further payments of 100 marks each year. Orkney and Shetland remained part of Norway until 1468.

It is a curious story. Scotland got a hold of Orkney and Shetland by means of a mortgage for 58,000 crowns. This was the unpaid balance of the dowry of the daughter, Margaret, of King Christian of Norway, who married James III of Scotland. Norway and Denmark have both tried to redeem them, even up to the time of Charles II, and could probably claim them even now. Scotland, and now Great Britain, however, having got the islands, has kept them.

I came to Sandwood to see Reay Forest in a right perspective. The tracks which traverse it are too close to the heights to let the traveller realise the pattern of the hills.

The Norse influence fades as the high ground is reached. The Norsemen, who began to arrive about 870, settled on the low coastal lands and the fertile strips which run up the valleys. Here in the lowlands, the place names still keep their Norse flavour; on the mountain heights, the names are mainly the Gaelic of the native Celts, who were pushed up into the hills by the invaders.

Celt and Norse strains intermingled. No women were allowed on the Viking ships, and the invaders took Celtic wives. The Celts were not seafaring folk; the Norse element gave birth to the strain of tough seamen that are bred on the West Highland coasts. All the terms dealing with boats in Gaelic are borrowed from the Norse. And what has been called the "vituperative vocabulary" is also Norse—doubtless the names that the invaders applied to the natives! One very bad name that one may call a person in Gaelic is *Uilbh* which is only the Norse word for a wolf—*ulf*.

Here at Sandwood, with the marks of the recent war beside me, I tried to picture the Norse ships riding in on the tide and being pulled up on the long sandy stretch between the rocky headlands. Perhaps as I did, they would come on a dull morning when the mist lay thick and still on the hills, and faint primrose flickers of sunlight tried to break through on the low ground. The sun grew stronger and the mist began to rise higher.

I left Sandwood, with its sandy beach and the freshwater loch behind the shingle bar, and going past the empty shepherd's house, struck back over the dark, bare moor, to Oldshore and Blairmore. The folk from these crofting townships were now out and busy on their peat-cuttings in the moor; their cattle were farther afield, almost at Sandwood, searching out the best bites of grass.

As the sun came out and the mist lifted, Reay forest appeared in the distance. The three mighty peaks of Foinaven, Arkle and Ben Stack rose suddenly from the undulating moor, Foinaven holding a last plume of cloud, which suddenly lifted, and showed the mountain's glittering spine of white quartzite. The low moor, the sudden peaks, the distant mass of Ben More Assynt to the south, the red sandstone of the cliffs of Sandwood, and the banded rock of the low moorland, this is part of a story far older than the Norsemen's coming.

Everywhere, the rocky floor below the surface skin of soil and trees and flowers, determines the sort of life that can be lived in any one place, and the form of the scenery that will be found. In the North-West Highlands, the geology not only gives rise to country of a strange beauty, but is also of great interest in itself. For geologists, this district, particularly Assynt, is classic ground.

In this North-Western country, there are four main units which build the different hill shapes. Oldest of all, oldest rock group in the world, is the Lewisian gneiss. On it, rests the Torridon sandstone, much younger and yet itself very old also. Neither formations have any fossils and we do not know if any living thing then walked upon the earth. The next formation, the Cambrian, contains fossils of various marine creatures, and since many of them are highly developed, it is supposed that life had existed on the earth a good time before the Cambrian rocks were laid down. Here, in the North-West, the Cambrian rocks are represented by shining white quartzites, once sandstones, and a series of limestones. It is the Cambrian quartzite which tops Arkle and Foinaven and Stack and makes them glint and shine in the sun.

The three formations are separated from each other by junctions called unconformities. This kind of junction indicates a vast spread of time between the making of the underlying rock type and the depositing of the overlying one on top of it. The Lewisian was in its present state and formed land when Torridon sandstone was laid on it, as sandy and gravelly deposits washed down from the mountains. Both Torridonian and Lewisian were plunged below the sea and levelled off by the waves before the Cambrian quartzites were laid down on them.

But the North-West Highlands would not be famous if that was all their geological history. They are famous not for static rocks but for moving rocks. After the Cambrian rocks had been laid down and consolidated, there came a series of vast movements, which thrust forward great slabs of rock and piled them up, over-riding older rocks on younger rocks. Thinking these thrust masses were in their natural order of succession, the early investigators were given many headaches in trying to understand the North-West Highland geology! It was the Knockan crag in Assynt which finally gave the full story away.

Last and greatest of these thrusts is the Moine thrust, which brings forward the great series of schists called the Moine schists, over Lewisian, Torridonian and Cambrian. This great thrust runs on a sinuous line, from Whitten Head on the North Coast between Tongue and Durness, to Sleat in Skye. Its present outcrop is therefore 120 miles long. The width of the zone of thrusts varies from twelve miles across in Skye, to seven in Assynt and one in Sutherland. In some parts of Ross it is represented only by a single thrust plane. The thrust dips gently to the east-south-east, and the minimum distance through which the rocks are known to have been shifted is ten miles.

It is not known, of course, which way the rocks moved: whether the pressure came from the south-south-east and piled up the rocks on the fringe of a strong stable area, or whether from the west-north-west and the western rocks moved south-south-east and let the Moine schists ride over them.

But throughout the North-West Highlands, these four formations determine the scenery. The origin of the names they have been given is interesting. The Lewisian was called after the island of Lewis, which is built up of this sort of rock. The Torridonian was called after Torridon in Ross-shire, where it is well developed. The Cambrian was named in Wales, where it is largely developed. The Moine schists were called after the Moine by Tongue, where they are well seen; Moine is merely the Gaelic for a peat moss. Nobody knows just where the Moine schists belong in the geological succession: some people would put them with the Torridonian and regard them as Torridon rocks which have undergone alteration into crystalline schists.

There are two rocks in the sea off Cape Wrath. One is A'Chailleach (the Old Woman), and the other Am Bodach (the Old Man). To me, the Lewisian, of the low moorland around Loch Inchard and Scourie, is essentially feminine, essentially *A'Chailleach*. Scottish geologists mapping the country for the first time, called the Lewisian many names. They called it Lewisian, they called it Archean, they called it the

Fundamental Complex, and, worst insult of all, they called it The Old Boy. Am Bodach for the delicate air of the Lewisian! Am Bodach for the lily pools and the grey slopes hung with golden gorse and the yellow scented tangle on the rocks of the sea lochs! They wrote their memoirs of the North-West Highlands, and they described the scenery about this Scourie district as "monotonous". It is a most colossal libel.

I admit that coming round by the coast road from Tongue and Durness into the Lewisian country is a distinctly puzzling experience. The gneiss is in little hillocks, all much of a height and intensely smoothed off and rounded by the ice of the Ice Age. It stays that way in all its outcrop here; one expects something to happen to the scenery and it doesn't. It remains the same, rather quiet, very desolate and empty of people, dark with peat bogs.

But it is a country of fascination. Each little crag is not the exact replica of the next. This one is smooth and that one is craggy, and between them lie lochans and tarns, where the lilies grow and the fish rise and spread slow ripple rings. And then the gneiss itself, hard, crystalline, flashing in the sun in the road cuttings, like a gypsy woman's eyes. Grey and white and black, green and red, the gneiss with its different minerals, is a pattern of colour; colour that needs to be looked for at close quarters perhaps, but which for brilliance is hard to beat. The Old Boy indeed! She is my Lady of the Little Lochs.

CHAPTER XVII

JOURNEY IN THE MIST

"TRAVELLING, it must be owned, is difficult and disagreeable, there being no roads, but such as the feet of men and cattle have made."

Thus wrote the minister of Edderachylis in 1793, in the old *Statistical Account of Scotland*. Of the mountain mass of Reay Forest, he said: "The more inland parts, which constitute Lord Reay's deer forest, are nothing but a vast group of dreadful mountains, with their summits piercing the clouds, and divided only by deep and very narrow vallies, whose declivities are so rugged and steep, as to be dangerous to travellors not furnished with guides."

There run two deep passes through Reay Forest, the mountain mass in the north-west corner of Scotland. Both open out of the deep hollow of Strath More in which lies Loch Hope. The more northern is the Bealach na Feithe; the more southern, the Bealach nam Meirleach. Both lead into the great cross-Scotland furrow along which runs the road from Laxford Bridge to Bonar Bridge.

The Bealach nam Meirleach is a drove route and right-of-way; the Bealach na Feithe is a well-kept stalker's path, which may be freely used in the non-shooting season, and with permission in the stalking season. From Lone on Loch Stack, the path can be followed right across the Forest to Gobernuisgach Lodge and a return made, on another stalking path, by Glen Golly and over the tops at 1,750 feet, between Creagan Meall

Horn and Foinaven, and back to Lone over the shoulder of Arkle. It is a long 20 miles, and it needs a fine day, when from the heights one could look down on the loch-studded lowland of the Lewisian gneiss. I chose to traverse it in dense mist and heavy rain, alone and without the guides so beloved of the ministers who wrote the *Statistical Accounts*.

It was a bad morning with low mist and driving sheets of rain. But the wind was blowing enough to keep the mist moving, and there were patches in the cloud through which one could see the sky. The day before, at Sandwood, a much more unpromising day had turned into one of clear views and hot sunshine. I made certain that the path was clearly marked all the way, but not—for I never gave them a thought—whether there were bridges on the bigger burns; for mist on a strange hill is hardly inviting when one has to depend on compass readings.

At Lone, one is on the edge of the country unaffected by the great thrusting movements. There are rugged little knolls of Lewisian gneiss and on them rests the Cambrian. Arkle shows the succession beautifully from across Loch Stack: the low knolls and bosses of the gneiss and above them the sharp line of contact and the pink-white screes of quartzite. Arkle itself, a great ridge of quartzite is involved in the thrusts and built of thrust-upon-thrust masses of Cambrian quartzite. The great Moine thrust runs east of it, and as I went up the steep incline into the beginning of the Bealach na Feithe, I crossed over it into hills of Moine schist—big, rather grassy hills with little crops of grey rock.

The Bealach na Feithe is a very easy pass. One goes up the long, broad, grassy valley of the Srath Luib na Seilich, then climbs steeply out at the top to a haggy col and drops down another broad valley—the Srath Coir'an Easaidh to Gober-nuisgach. The crossing is made at a height of 1,471 feet, and the path is good, with bridges over the streams, all the way.

The name Bealach na Feithe seems to refer to the meandering streams which wind at the bottom of these two broad valleys. *Bealach* means a pass or a hollow, *Feithe* is a slowly moving stream.

The weather played its well-known trick of appearing to clear and then becoming worse when one is well committed to the full journey. As I climbed into the pass, I caught little glimpses of Ben Stack, opposite Arkle across Loch Stack, and as I came down upon the other side, I made out the lower half of Ben Hope above Loch Hope, and the sun was warm to feel. Then, as I turned up Glen Golly, and headed for the higher return journey, the sun retired into the clouds, the mist came lower and it began to spit with rain.

Reay is an ancient and famous forest, and as I walked along I saw a number of herds of red deer. Sir Robert Gordon, writing in 1630, of this country, describes the different sorts of game found therein. He says:

All these forrests and schases are verie profitable for feiding of bestiall and delectable for hunting. They are full of reid-deir and roes, woulffs, foxes, wyld catts, brocks, skuyrells, whittrets, weasels, otters, martrixes, hares and fumarts. In these forrests, and in all this province, ther is great store of partridges, pluivers, capercalegs, blackwaks, murefowls, heth-hens, swanes, bewters, turtle-doves, herons, dowes, steares or starlings, lair-igigh or knag (which is a foull lyke unto a paroket or parret, which maks place for her nest with her beck in the oak trie), duke, draig, widgeon, teale, wild gouse, ringouse, routs, whaips, shot-whaips, woodcock, larkes, sparrows, snyps, blackburds or osills, meireis, thrushes, and all other kinds of wild-foule and birds, which are to be had in any pairt of this kingdom.

Game begets poachers. There was a famous poacher in this country who lived at Durness, by name John More (Big John). One day, the rightful owner of the deer which John so often troubled, Donald Lord Reay, decided to call upon John and try to put a stop to his poaching habits. Leaving his followers, he called alone and asked John for some breakfast. "Come in", said John, "and sit on my stool, and you will get to eat what cost me some trouble in collecting."

John quickly got a good meal ready. He laid the rough table with some remarkably fine dinner napkins, cooked a fine grilse (relating that it had come out of one of Lord Reay's rivers) and a breast of a deer, and brought forth some smuggled brandy with which to wash down the meats.

My Lord must needs ask for salt and a knife, to which John retorted "that teeth and hands were of little use, if they could not master dead fish and flesh; that the deer seasoned their flesh with salt on the hill, whilst the herring could not do so in the sea; and that the salmon, like the Durness butter, was better without salt".

When he had eaten a good meal, Lord Reay attempted to bargain with John. Said he, "I am well pleased that although you invade the property of others, you do not conceal the truth, and that you have freely given me the best entertainment that your depredations on my property have enabled you to bestow. I will, therefore, allow you to go occasionally to Foinaven in search of a deer, if you will engage not to interfere with deer, or any sort of game, in any other part of my forest."

"Donald," said John, "you may put Foinaven in your paunch, for wherever the deer are, there will John More be found."

The path up Glen Golly is less well kept than that through the Bealach na Feithe and is a narrow but quite distinct footpath through the heather. Glen Golly is a deep rocky glen through which a fair-sized river tumbles in waterfalls, shaded by a narrow strip of birchwood. There are no bridges on this path and when one leaves Glen Golly, the stream (like all the others) must be forded. In spate, this might give a little trouble; in the rain when I crossed, though the burns were not in spate, they were distinctly wetting to get over.

From the crossing of the Glen Golly river, the path can be seen snaking up a hillside in a series of hairpin bends. These bends I found very trying for there seemed to be no end to them. As soon as one thought that the last was reached, another hove in sight. In clear weather, there would be a very fine view back down Glen Golly and of the Reay hills upon either side.

For a Highland glen, Golly seems a curious name. Its Gaelic spelling (with the same pronounciation) is *Gollaidh*, and it comes from a word *Goll*, blind. It means a glen in which the stream is "blind" or buried in trees. To-day the trees only form a narrow fringe along the gorge; perhaps once the woods were much more extensive, for the famous Gaelic bard of Sutherland, Rob Donn, wrote a poem called "Gleann Gollaidh nan Craobh" (Glen Golly of Trees).

But I was leaving the glen behind and going up into the mist. The sun made a final weak attempt to break through; then the mist thickened about Meall Horn, which lay to my left, and the rain began to drive across the boggy flat on which the hairpin climb ends. On this flat, which lies about the 1,400 foot contour, are little dark tarns, through which the track twists. I remember that bogbean was growing on some of the tarns, but the driving rain was increasing, and with a strong wind behind it, was almost blinding.

The way drops again, climbs up another low ridge, past another tarn and then goes steeply down into the glen of the Allt an Easain Ghil—the stream (*allt*) of the hollow (Norse, *gill*) of the waterfall. The valley is steep upon both sides, steepest to the north-west where it rises almost sheerly up, and a stream drops down it in a series of white cascades. Down the rocky valley, there is a glimpse into Strath Dionard, with Loch Dionard cradled below high crags. Up the glen, a little above the path crossing, the burn flows out of a dark pool, cupped below mighty crags. This is An Dubh-Lochan—the little black pool. Down the crags, another waterfall pours into the lochan, from a second and smaller lochan in another rocky cup at the top of the crag. This is the Wolf Lochan (Lochan Ulabhath). Behind it again, rise more dark crags to the 2,548 foot summit of Meall Horn.

This place is very interesting geologically and here the complicated relations of the thrust rocks are very well seen. The Moine thrust is well exposed along the shoulder of Meall Horn called Creagan Meall Horn. The thrust schists give rise to the sudden rise of the crag above the Cambrian rocks to the north which make up the Plat Reidh, and which are themselves involved in the lowest thrust of the series, called the Sole. Between the thrust masses brought forward by the sole and the Moine thrust, is a third called the Arnaboll thrust, which brings forward Lewisian gneiss in the country east of the Plat Reidh. It is probable that the Arnaboll thrust plane extended over the Plat Reidh, and that the level surface of the Plat is due to the recent weathering-off of the rocks that were thrust over it.

For me, it was far too wet to stop to look at these various rocks properly, and I scurried up the path on the slope of Plat Reidh. It goes up beside the waterfall, and from across the valley looked almost sheer, yet I found it less tiring than the hairpins out of Glen Golly. The map shows the path ending on the Plat Reidh and another path starting on the farther side of Creagan Meall Horn, but these two have recently been joined by a new path, so that the way is clear.

The Plat Reidh is really the broad end of the long narrow ridge of Foinaven of the glittering quartzites. Its name, properly Foinne bheinn, means white mountain. On its top is found the rare Curved Woodrush (*Luzula arcuata*) and also the Northern Rock cress (*Arabis petrae*). The *New Statistical Account* claims (in 1834) that Foinaven, Ben More Assynt and Braeriach are the only Scottish mountains to have the Curved Woodrush.

But it is possibly to be found on some few others of the higher tops. Foinaven rises to 2,980 feet. The ridge sweeps back to the Plat Reidh and round under Creagan Meall Horn, to jut out again in the ridge of Arkle.

The path to Lone gives a great view down into the arcuate hollow which lies between these two great mountains of Cambrian quartzite, a hollow edged by great crags and floored by small lakes.

As I padded along above the drop down into the hollow between Foinaven and Arkle, the mist clearing slightly as I began to lose height and go down toward Lone, I was able, if not to take full advantage of the view, to observe the fact that the rain with the wind behind it, had gone through my mackintosh and my supposedly weatherproof jacket but not through the heavy tartan of my kilt, and observe also upon mist in mountains.

Mist adds much to mountains. It takes away their colour and their views, but it gives them added height (for is the top you see the real summit or a mere spur seen against the mist bank?) and it gives them added size and it gives them mystery. The smallest glen in the mist will appear a great valley leading up into some undiscovered fairyland. There is no telling what lies behind the mist wreaths. Here surely is the birthplace of some of the stories of sprites and kelpies. The burn seems to roar with a fuller voice, maybe a water-bull is roaring with it. Something indefinite scrabbles away; it may be a deer, but you cannot see—it may be not. This very morning, driving to Lone, I saw white smoke in the distance, only to find, when I got closer, that it was the side of a white-washed house!

Mist then may mean fear—the wild, unreasoning fear of the unknown, the fears that modern man tries to put behind him. Fear of the supernatural, fear of the old, half-forgotten gods, fear of the unknown, for the unknown is always more terrible than the known. And, too, there may be the real practical fear of getting lost, which a map and a compass alone can fight. Most people's sense of direction, when the landmarks are hidden, takes them round in right-handed circles.

"In the Diri-more", wrote Sir Robert Gordon, "ther is a hill called Arkill; all the deir that ar bred therein, or haunt within the bounds of that hill, have forked taills, thrie inches long, whereby they are easailie known and decerned from all other deir."

As I came down over the shoulder of Arkle and into a deep green valley of the Allt Horn, which drops in a "mare's tail" waterfall out of the glen down to Lone at Loch Stack, a big herd of red deer on the opposite slope sighted me, and began to move off uphill. Had they forked tails? They were too far away to see, and a dead one in the Bealach na Feithe was rather past the time for examination.

I see no reason why deer should not have forked tails. A forked tail could quite well arise as a "sport" and be perpetuated for some time. There is another old tale of deer with forked tails on a certain hill in Lewis. The writer of the account of the parish of Edderachyllis in the *New Statistical Account* claimed that the Arkle deer still had forked tails. That was in 1840. I asked the keeper at Airdachuilinn about the tails. He said he had cut up plenty of Arkle deer and never seen one with a forked tail. But when they are moulting, said he, the hair may thin on the tail and part into two tufts which might give rise to the story. But that might apply equally to all deer and not to particular deer on a hill in Lewis and a hill in Reay Forest. Perhaps a forked tail did occur and then died out. Perhaps it is merely a traveller's tale.

The path drops down in steep bends to Lone and the good track back to the high road at Achfary. Nobody lives at Lone now, the nearest house is the keeper's, almost a mile farther on, at Airdachuilinn. Once, however, people did live at Lone, and there is a grim and rather bloody story told about one of them.

There was a hunting lodge belonging to the MacKays on an island in Loch Stack. When the Laird arrived there for his hunting, the population used to come to the island with various gifts, mostly of food of various sorts. Once, when Sir Hugh MacKay of Far, who was the father of Donald, the first Lord Reay, came to the island, he was strongly attracted by a young woman from Lone who came, as was the custom, with gifts of milk and cheese. She, however, refused his advances and said she would have nothing to do with any man while her husband lived. MacKay was set on his purpose and held her prisoner on the island, going next day, with a body of men to Lone.

They called out the woman's husband and asked him to come with them. As they went along, one man fell back and stabbed the unfortunate victim in the back. They then cut off his head and carried it back to his wife on the island. There was now nothing for it but for the woman to let Sir Hugh have his way. She became the mother of Donald MacKay, who was the first MacKay to be laird of Edderachyllis.

This Donald MacKay was also something of a tough customer and he got Edderachyllis by anything but lawful means. James MacLeod was then the Laird of Edderachyllis, but his cousin Donald MacLeod, Donald MacKay and the Morrisons of Durness and Ashir contrived to slay both James and his friends. The two Donalds had arranged to share Edderachyllis between them, and that MacLeod should also marry the woman of Lone, MacKay's mother. When it came to the point, however, of dividing the spoil, Donald MacKay must needs take all Edderachyllis for himself and poor Donald MacLeod had to make do with the woman and the Davoch of Hope!

Donald MacLeod is buried in the wall of Durness Church. In his old age, he was taunted by an old woman that she would dance on his grave. Donald was furious, and agreed to build up a wall of the church on condition that his body should be placed in a niche in it. He died in 1623, and the inscription reads:

> Donald Mhic Mhorchaidh Heir lys lo
> Vas il to his friend, var to his fo
> True to his maister in veird and vo.

Many stories are told of him. He is said to have committed eighteen murders. He was a great poacher and a great shot with the bow. Although his family name was MacLeod, his Gaelic patronymic by which he would be usually known, was Donald 'ic Mhorchaidh 'ic Ian Mhor (Donald son of Murdoch son of Big John).

When Donald was an old man, the minister, Mr. Alexander Munro, saw him and tried to persuade him to repent of his evil ways. Donald was then too infirm to murder Munro on the spot, but sent his two sons after him with instructions not to appear before him again without the minister's heart. However, the minister was not alone and the man with him had a gun, so MacLeod's two sons thought better of the project. Still, old Donald would have to be faced. They accordingly, killed a sheep and brought back its heart. "Ha", said Donald MacLeod when he saw it, "I always thought the Munros cowards, but never knew till now that they had the heart of a sheep!"

CHAPTER XVIII

THE ROBBERS' PASS

THE Bealach nam Meirleach—the Robbers' Pass—links the valley of Strath More with that of Loch More and Loch Shin, and is the only right-of-way through the Reay Forest. Certainly it is a drove road, but whether it was particularly frequented by thieves, I have not been able to find out.

Strictly speaking, I suppose one should begin the through route on the shores of the sea loch of Eriboll on the North Coast of Scotland. Here the place names are mostly Norse. Eriboll is *Eyrr-bol* (beach town). Eastward from Eriboll lies the great peat moss called the Moine, after which the Moine schists were named. Beyond the Moine is Tongue. Tongue is Norse too, *Tunga* meaning a tongue of land. The Norsemen called it by another name too—Kirkiboll (the church town) But in Gaelic Tongue is *Ceann-t-saile a'mhic-aoidh*—the head of the salt water.

From Loch Eriboll, the way goes along the long, narrow fresh-water loch, Hope, under the great mass of Ben Hope. Again the name is Norse, *hop* (a bay). I suppose they called the bay on Loch Eriboll, *hop*, where the river from Loch Hope enters the sea, and that the name slowly worked its way inland, first being applied to the river, then to the loch and finally to the mountain above the loch.

Ben Hope (3,040 ft.) is the most northerly peak over 3,000 feet in the British Isles. It rises nearly its full height above Loch Hope, for the loch is only about twelve feet above sea level, and the hill rears itself above it in two great terrace features. It is carved out of the Moine schists; it is possible that the great escarpment at 2,000 feet may be due to a thrust plane affecting these schists.

At the south end of Loch Hope, a beautiful natural birch wood hangs on the lower, or 1,000 foot escarpment, and reaches down to the narrow plat between lochside and crag along which the little track-like road from Altnaharra to Hope goes.

Advancing southward, one enters the broad Strath More (Gaelic, the big open valley), a place of level green marshy flats, where the cotton grass spreads white fluffy carpets. Above the level flat, where the Strathmore river twists, rise the green hill slopes, broken here and there by grey rock. They rise steeply, the way is between the heights of Ben Hope and the northern foothills of Reay Forest. Down the 2,000 foot escarpment of Ben Hope, the Allt na Caillich (stream of the old woman) drops in a great waterfall to the few houses of Alltna-caillich, where rowan trees form a little grove about the settlement and scent all the roadway in the spring with their white bunches of flowers. The rowan is supposed to be a lucky tree to plant about the house, which it is supposed to protect from all manner of dangers.

A little farther up the strath, is the ruin of Dun Dornaigil, looking rather like a bishop's mitre shorn of one horn. It is a broch, one of the so-called Pictish towers.

"Dundornigil", relates a writer in *MacFarlane's Geographical Collections*, in an account dated 1726, is "an old building made in the form of a sugar loaff and with a double wall and winding stairs in the middle of the wall round about, and little places for men to ly in as is thought and all built of dry stone without any mortar." This is the typical broch described to the life. But Dun Dornaigil has fallen in greatly since that description was written and now consists of a circular wall, rising to a

The Broch of Dun Dornaigil, Strath More, Reay Forest

Tree root preserved in iron slag, Fasagh, Loch Maree

high point above the entrance, the interior being completely blocked with fallen stones. It is now impossible to see the passages in the thickness of the wall.

The most interesting feature of Dun Dornaigil is the huge triangular slab of schist which forms the lintel of the low doorway. Triangular lintels have been found in several brochs, and must have been some sort of fashion or fancy, for they must have been quite hard to make and set up.

The slab sits with the base of the triangle forming the actual lintel, and the apex jutting up above the door. My rough measurements gave the thickness of the slab as 8 inches, the base as 58 inches, the height from base to apex as 36 inches, and the two sides of the triangular as 43 inches.

The name broch, by the way, is from the old Norse word *borg* (a castle). It is the same word as the old English *burgh*, our modern borough, or in Scotland, *burgh*, which has developed in meaning from the castle/stronghold idea into one of a civic community.

Beyond Dun Dornaigil, the rough little motoring road climbs up the side of the strath and heads away over the moors past Loch Meadie to Altnaharra. The Bealach nam Meirleach right-of-way leaves it, at an empty house called Achfary, and follows the track to Gobernuisgach Lodge. There the ways divide: to the right, up Glen Golly; in the middle, up the Bealach na Feithe; to the left, the right-of-way, the Bealach nam Meirleach.

This track, which cuts off a very long way round, used to be passable for motors, but has now been let go. It was a well-made track, raised above the hollows of the moor, with bridges over the streams and little milestones of blocks of schist along its verge. Mr. Scobie, the keeper at Airdachuilinn, told me that he thought he was the last person to take a vehicle over it. The vehicle was a motor cycle combination, and the time, some fifteen years ago. He was going to a clay-

pigeon shoot at Altnaharra. From the keeper's house on Loch
Stack, Altnaharra is only about 30 miles by the Bealach nam
Meirleach; by the present main road via Lairg, it is about 50
miles.

The Bealach runs entirely through mountains carved in the
Moine schists. The hills are generally rather rounded, though
they have many crops of grey rock showing through the turf,
and some craggy places. The schists here are technically called
siliceous granulites. They represent impure sandstones which
have been recrystallised and converted into schists by the
influence of heat and pressure.

The path winds under the rather craggy height of the Sail
an Las, and joins the Allt a'Chraois, which it follows up into
the pass. The way lies between the mountain mass of the Sail
an Las, Beinn Direach and Meall a'Chleirich (the round hill
of the clergyman) and the great mass of Ben Hee. Ben Hee
is the southern termination of Reay forest's mountains. It
rises to 2,864 feet, and is made up of several connected hills,
which have their own special names. Ben Hee is rather the
name of the group: it means the Mountain of the Fairies.

The Allt a'Chraois flows out of a chain of little lochs which
lie between these mountains along the floor of the pass. They
are Loch an Aslaird, into which the Allt an Aslaird falls in a
beautiful series of cascades, Loch an t-Seilg and Loch an Tuim
Bhuidhe, at the head of the pass. These mean, respectively,
the lake of the request, the lake of hunting and the lake of the
yellow hillock. Above the lochs rise the slopes of Ben Hee,
with silver outcrops of rock. When I saw them they were wet
with rain and the mist was low. It parted suddenly and re-
vealed the wet shining rocks. The lochs are edged with little
beaches of deep yellow sand. The heather slopes were a deep
red-brown, intermixed with yellow reedy grass and verdant
patches of green turf. The moving mist first outlined a trail
of fantastic fallen boulders on the shoulder of Meall a'Chleirich,

then thickened with the coming of another shower. The lochs were dull, leaden mirrors. Suddenly, as the rain struck, there was a loud hissing, splashing sound, and the lochs were alive with silver balls of rain leaping in the air as they struck the water.

Leaving the lochs, one climbs a little, into a country of peat hags, lying on a col between the high mountains, and then goes gently down, through a moorland strip, still between the high hills, to Loch Merkland. In June there were a few marsh orchids, the pink lousewort and the blue mountain milkwort to be seen along the track, and I noticed a strong smell of fox at several places!

The top of the pass is just over the 800-foot contour line, and lies on the watershed between the streams draining to Loch Hope and the North Coast, and the streams draining into Loch Merkland and the East Coast.

The track keeps fairly close to a medium-sized stream, called the Highlandman's burn—Allt nan Albannach. This stream rises among the heights of Beinn Direach and Carn Tionail and is joined by burns from the corrie loch of Loch Ulbhach and from the heights of Ben Hee. There are rather attractive little cascades on all these burns.

Mention of corrie lochs reminds that the mountains of the Reay Forest are noted for their fine corries—usually holding a small lake. These corries are great hollows scooped out of the hillside by the ice in the waning stages of the Ice Age, when the remaining glaciers clung to the Reay heights. A rough count on the map gives the number of the high-level lochs in Reay Forest as about 20; all of them would be worth visiting.

The hollow of Loch Merkland, into which the Bealach nam Meirleach leads, extends right across Scotland. It forms an easy crossing of the country from east to west, and along it runs the present road from Bonar Bridge at the head of the Dornoch Firth on the East Coast, to Laxford Bridge at the head of the sea loch Laxford on the West Coast.

The valley begins in Loch Laxford, one of the long, narrow fiords of the Western Highland coast, and into which flows the river Laxford. The river Laxford (Norse, Salmon ford) rises out of Loch Stack and runs a short course to the sea through a gorge in the Lewisian gneiss. It is a famous salmon river.

The valley continues through the hollow of Loch Stack to the long narrow loch of Loch More. This is a beautiful sheet of water lying among the high green hills of the Reay Forest, the road running along its south-western shore, fringed with birches. In 1726, there were said to be growing on both sides of Loch More plenty of "tall birks, elms, allers and other tymber". Virtually all this natural forest is now missing.

The road climbs into a low pass beyond Loch More. The col, between steep hillsides, is only 470 feet above sea level. It rises like a little hump between Loch More and Loch Merkland. It is the main watershed of Scotland, the streams upon one side falling to the West Coast, and those upon the other, to the East Coast.

Loch Merkland is another long narrow loch amongst the high Reay hills. I was told that it was noted for its water spouts. A little farther down the valley is Loch a'Ghriama, a much smaller loch, linked by a short stream with the head of Loch Shin.

Loch Shin is the largest loch in Scotland north of the Great Glen. It is the fifth longest stretch of water in Scotland ($17\frac{1}{4}$ miles) being exceeded only by Lochs Awe, Ness, Lomond and Shiel. It lies in a great valley with smooth green hill slopes rising from the water, and with, across their tops, a glimpse of the mass of Ben More Assynt. Lairg lies at its farther end, and the River Shin continues along the course of the great cross-country furrow, to its end in the Dornoch Firth.

The lochs in this great valley seem to be mainly rock basins. They are hollows which were over-deepened and hollowed out by the ice moving through the glen during the Ice Age. But the great hollow itself is much older than the time of the ice sheets.

These cross-Scotland valleys, which form the easy routes across the north-south mountain chain (Drum Alban) were formed when the river system of this part of the country was rather different from its present state. Although the rocks now exposed in the North-West Highlands are very ancient; they were once covered by much younger rocks, which have now been all weathered off. The Western Isles are mere remnants of a once much more extensive land, on which were poured out the great flows of lava and other igneous rocks, which are still to be seen in the Isles and on the West Coast in Argyllshire.

This more extensive tract of land seems to have sloped gently to the south-east. Down this slope flowed great rivers into the sea which lay from the north of France to Schleswig Holstein (the Miocene Sea). These rivers cut the cross-Scotland valleys, of which the Laxford-Shin hollow is an example. Later on, the land which lay where the Minch now flows, foundered, and reversed the direction of the drainage at the head of the valley. This brought about the present state of affairs, where there are long eastward-flowing streams flowing along the old consequent valleys, and short westward-flowing obsequent streams on the other side of the present watershed. The valley and its stream is called consequent because it results directly from the slope of the original land surface.

The further development of the Highland drainage system was controlled directly by the grain of the present rocks, which were, by then, exposed to denudation. Deep valleys were also excavated along lines of breakage and crushing. In the Reay country, the straight, deep gorge of Golly Glen has been excavated along a line of crushing and breakage in the schists.

M

It is because of these old consequent valleys that one can drive across Scotland, east to west, without climbing over the 1,000 foot contour, without effort, almost without touching the gear lever. But heaven help the man who walks through these gorges with a heavy pack on a hot day on the hard metalled road!

Mention may be made here of some of the other through valleys. There is the one from Dingwall through by Achnasheen to Strath Carron. Another is up Glen Moriston to Loch Duich, another from Invergarry to Kinloch Hourn. All these routes carry present-day motor roads; the first mentioned also carries the railway from Inverness to Kyle of Lochalsh. Road and rail also share the through valley from Fort William up Loch Eil to Arisaig.

X

THE ROAD FROM THE ISLES

CHAPTER XIX

SOUTHWARD FROM THE GREAT GLEN

WHEN the trade in Highland black cattle was at its height, it was a long road that some of the droves took. The old *Statistical Account* for Harris (1794) states that some 200 cattle were sold each year and driven south, some to Southern Scotland but mostly to England. Lewis, in 1765, sold cattle to the value of £1430, 700 beasts in all but of these 300 were salted carcases, and 100 sold to shipping coming into Stornoway. The remaining 300 went on the hoof.

For Harris and Lewis, and the rest of the Outer Hebrides, Skye was the stepping-stone to the mainland roads. The beasts were ferried to Skye and then swum from Skye to the mainland. Martin Martin (*A Description of the Western Islands of Scotland*, 1695) describes the crossing to Glenelg from Skye:

They begin when it is near low water and fasten a twisted with about the lower jaw of each cow. The other end of the with is fastened to another cow's tail; and the number so tied together is commonly five. A boat with four oars rows off, and a man sitting the stern holds the with in his hand to keep up the foremost cow's head; and thus all the five cows swim as fast as the boat rows; and in this manner above a hundred may be ferried over in one day. These cows are sometimes drove about 400 miles further south. They soon grow fat, and prove sweet and tender beef.

It must have been a long journey from the Isles to the

south, for the cattle only walked about ten miles a day. From Skye they made either over Mam Ratagain or by Kinloch Hourn and Glengarry to the Great Glen—routes which have already been described. The routes which they followed south from the Great Glen may now be briefly indicated.

Cattle droving as such is only lately dead in the Highlands. Whilst the big trade in black cattle became important toward the end of the seventeenth century and slowly decreased with the development of the sheep walks; droving and the drove roads remained the sole means of moving animals from one place to another until the coming of the railway and the motor cattle truck. The drovers, a man who remembered them told me, used to wear a Highland plaid with their supply of meal tied up in a corner of it. Mixed with whisky and sugar, this oatmeal made a form of Atholl brose which would be a warming meal on a wet night on a cold road.

From the Great Glen, itself the most important and easiest east-west route across the Scottish Highlands, cattle going to England had two great mountain barriers to cross, the Grampian Highlands and the Southern Uplands of the Border country.

The Grampians, of course, are a ghost name, a map-maker's misreading of Mons Graupius, the place where the Caledonians were defeated by Agricola in A.D. 84. The Caledonians were led by one Calgacus, which is rendered in *Tacitus* as Galgacus. This has led to the suggestion (by the late Professor Watson) that Mons Graupius was really Mons Craupius and may perhaps refer to Duncrub near Perth.

So that the name Grampian, originally applied to a small hill near Perth has probably undergone two misreadings, and come to be applied to the mountain massif between the Great Glen and the Midland Valley by a series of errors. In fact, there is not one mountain mass but two. Drum Albyn, the chain of hills running from south to north up the west side of

IN THE HEART OF THE GREAT GLEN

Loch Lochy and the slopes of Sran a' Choire
Gharbh above Kilfinnan. The old right of way
runs on the farther side of the loch from
Kilfinnan to Loch Arkais : the modern main
road upon the near side.

the Highlands is the most important, and has always influenced the course of Highland history. It was Drum Albyn which separated the Scots of Dalradia from the Picts.

A much more easily turned line is the east-west range, which extends from Drum Albyn to the lowlands of Banff and Aberdeen and whose proper name is not Grampian but the Mounth. The Mounth is readily crossed by the Pass of Drumochter or by the Mounth road passes farther east. It can be easily turned by the eastern lowlands, and it was this east coast route which the Roman legions took when they marched north, and later, St. Ninian on his missionary journeys to the north of Scotland.

The cattle from the Isles had the choice of routes when they reached the Great Glen, either to cross the Mounth by Drumochter or to weave in and out of the hills of Drum Albyn. Their destination was often the big cattle fair at Crieff. At this Michaelmas tryst, sometimes 30,000 cattle were sold. About 1770, it was transferred to Falkirk. The English buyers came to these fairs and sometimes hired the Scottish drovers to take their purchases across the Border.

From the Isles and the North-West Highlands, there were, therefore, two main lines of drove roads, one by Corrieyairack and Drumochter, and the other by Glen Coe and Tyndrum to Callander.

Cattle coming from Skye by way of the road over Mam Ratagain and Glen Moriston to Fort Augustus could then cross Corrieyairack and head into Drumochter from Dalwhinnie. The Corrieyairack route, going up the Tarff valley and crossing over, at 2,507 feet, to the headquarters of the Spey, was made into a military road by General Wade in 1731. It was the highest made road in Britain and a useful link, since it avoids the long detour which people in the Fort Augustus district have to make by Inverness or Fort William when they wish to go south. The Corrieyairack route is snowed up during winter, but it is a great pity that it has been allowed to fall into disrepair.

Cattle from the west could also join the Fort Augustus-Corrieyairack-Dalwhinnie-Drumochter-Perth line by turning out of the Great Glen on Loch Lochy side and going up Glen Gloy by a track called the "soft road for the hoggs" to join the Corrieyairack road at Meallgarbha. This avoids the climb over the top of the Pass of Corrieyairack.

Bishop Forbes (who compiled the *Lyon in Mourning*) gives an interesting account of the cattle droves in the Pass of Drumochter. He was coming back from one of his episcopal visits to the north, and on 31st August 1762, counted eight droves of black cattle going to Crieff tryst and numbering some 1,200 beasts. They were from Skye, and a MacQueen who was in charge told the Bishop that

They had four or five Horses with Provisions for themselves by the Way, particularly Blankets to wrap themselves in when sleeping in the open Air, as they rest upon the bleak Mountains, the heathy Moors, or the verdant Glens, just as it happens towards the Evening; that they tend their Flocks by night, and never move till about 8 in the Morning, and then march the Cattle at leisure, that they may feed a little as they go along. They rest a while at midday to take some Dinner, and so let the Cattle feed or rest as they please. The proprietor does not travel with the Cattle, but has One for his Deputy to command ye whole, and he comes to the place appointed against ye Day fixed for the Fair. When the Flock is very large, as the present, they divide it, though belonging to One, into several Droves, that they may not hurt one another in narrow Passes, particularly on Bridges, many of which they go along. Each drove had a particular number of men with some Boys to look after the Cattle.

The Bishop describes how: "On the dusky Muir of Drumochtir we had a full view of all the Cattle, from Rear to Front, which would take up about a Mile in length, and were greatly entertained in driving along through the midst of them, some of them skipping it away before us, like so many Deer. They were sleek, and in good Order, and fit for present Use."

Another route leading from the North-West on to the Drumochter-Perth line south is the "Road to the Isles". This goes by the Lairig Leacach through the mountains east of Ben Nevis, and then by Loch Treig and Loch Rannoch to join the main Inverness-Perth road.

The Lairig Leacach is entered from Spean Bridge, a track running up into the pass from Corriecoillie. The name means the Pass of the Flagstones. It was this way that Montrose went to defeat Argyll at Inverlochy. He left Fort Augustus and went up the Corrieyairack track, turned off it to go down Glen Roy, crossed the Spean, made up the Lairig and then down Glen Nevis to take Argyll completly by surprise. This march was made in February 1645 in the teeth of the winter weather.

Montrose crossed the Spean by the ford at Dalnabea near Corriecoillie and some little way above the present Spean Bridge. It was in 1736 that Wade completed High Bridge over the Spean. High Bridge took the place of the old ford and became the nodal point of the Great Glen tracks at this point. High Bridge was the place where a dozen Highlanders by dint of much shouting and running through the bushes contrived to turn back two companies of the Scots Royals who thought the bridge was held by a large force. Thus began the first skirmish of the '45, for the Royals were overtaken and defeated at Laggan while they were trying to beat a retreat back to Fort Augustus.

High Bridge is farther downstream than the modern Spean Bridge. It is now in ruin with only the piers intact. The river runs in a deep and rocky gorge at this point, deep pools alternating with shallower and more gravelly stretches; the crags wooded. The piers rise some 80 feet above the surface of the water and carried three arches, the middle one of which had a diameter of 50 feet and the two others of 40 feet. It cost £1087 6s. 8d. to build.

Cattle making for the Glen Coe-Tyndrum-Callander line could also go up the Lairig Leacach from High Bridge. From the head of Loch Treig, they turned up Gleann Iolairean and then down the Ciaran Water and on to Kingshouse at the top of Glen Coe. From there, the way was over the Moor of Rannoch to Tyndrum and by Glen Ogle to Callander, Stirling, Falkirk or Crieff.

Or Kingshouse could be reached from Fort William by Blairmachfoldach and Kinlochleven and the Devil's Staircase. This was made into the military road from Stirling to Fort William by Caulfield in 1751. The Devil's Staircase hairpin bends lead up from Altnafeadh in Glen Coe to cross between Stob Mhic Mhartuin and Beinn Bheag at a height of 1,800 feet; the route then turns towards the valley of the river Leven and descends to Kinlochleven, where are the graves of the soldiers who died during the construction of the road.

The Devil's Staircase part of the military road was abandoned some 30 years after it was made in favour of the easier line through the Pass of Glen Coe itself.

Going south from the Falkirk tryst, the cattle came into very different country. To-day, there are three mainroad crossings of the Border: by Berwick upon Tweed, by Carter Bar over the Cheviot ridge and by Carlisle. North of these crossings lie the mass of Border hills, the Southern Uplands, and the modern roads thread through them following the network of cross-country valleys.

The present roads are mostly made upon the lines of earlier trackways, but as in the Highlands, the Border hills have as well a great number of old trackways not now in use. The Cheviot crossings are perhaps the most striking case in point. There is now only the one road over the Cheviots, by Carter Bar, an ancient route formerly called the Redeswire. In 1543, however, there were listed 17 Cheviot crossings, including the Roman road, Dere Street, which crosses to the east of Carter Bar.

Not only have these tracks fallen out of use, but the population has moved away from these hills. One of the tracks over the Cheviots was the Wheel Causeway and on it stood the village of Wheel, of which not a stone remains but those of the church built into a sheep fank. It is a bleak, bare and boggy country, and one cannot but wonder whether there has been some change in the climate and whether once the slopes of the Cheviots were more fertile.

The Highland cattle must have found the going very different from the Highland tracks. The Border hills are essentially grassy or heathy uplands, broad swelling ridges without dramatic crags or frost-shattered peaks. Highland tracks thread through the valleys and as far as they possibly can avoid going over the tops of the mountains. In the Borders, the ridgeway appears. Here are grassy paths keeping to the tops of the mountain ridges, the land falling away upon either hand. The Minchmoor road from Peebles and Traquair to Selkirk is one of the finest examples. It is a grassy road keeping along the tops of hills at a height of well over 1,500 feet. On either side, there are great views across the Border country, northward and southward, in sharp contrast to the Highland tracks, which are often disappointing as a way of seeing the country, because they keep so much to the glens. The Pass of Corrieyairack, for all its climbing, will not give you as good a view of the country as an easy climb up one of the Great Glen hills.

Some of the Border roads are partly ridgeways and partly valley roads. There is a drove road which leads through the Borders from Falkirk and begins by crossing the Pentland Hills by the pass of the Cauldstane Slap. This is a very fine pass, with the two square hills of the Cairns rising upon either side of it. The track follows the Lyne Water down from the summit of the crossing to West Linton, and then goes by Romano, Green Knowe and Upper Stewarton to Peebles.

At Peebles, the droves could rest on the Kingsmuir which is now the railway station. Southward the track becomes a ridgeway, snaking up over Kailzie Hill and going over to Blackhouse and St. Mary's Loch by way of the heights of Birkscairn Hill (2,169 ft.). It then continued southward by Tushielaw, Hoscoteshiel and Robertson.

The Thieves Road is another famous Border ridgeway. It is said to be traceable from the Pentlands right through into Liddesdale on the Border. From a ford on the Tweed to the west of Peebles, it climbed over the hills to St. Mary's Loch as a ridgeway at a height of over 2,000 feet. It crosses Dollar Law which is 2,680 feet high. It goes next across the Ettrick Forest country to turn south near Hawick and go over the hills from the head of the Allan Water by Sire Knowe and Thiefsike Head to Liddesdale which it enters near Newcastleton.

The Thieves Road, whose name recalls the Bealach nam Meirleach in Reay Forest, Sutherland, was largely used by the Border reivers on their forays. And the cattle droves which used the Cauldstane Slap as they went south from Falkirk tryst were also going along a track which had earlier seen many herds of stolen cattle go by.

This then was the pattern of the road from the Outer Isles that the cattle took to England, the ferry to Skye, the swimming of the Kyle to the mainland, the Highland track through the mountains following the lower ground, the fertile plains of the Midland valley and the swelling uplands of the Borders with their ridgeways and sweet green turf. From the rocky cliffs and long sandy beaches backed by the primrose-spangled sand dunes of the Outer Isles, by the fiords of the West and the cliffs of Nevis, by the peat hags of Rannoch and the rock of Stirling Castle, by the peel towers and the green valleys of the Borders; the drove roads went south into England.

ON FOLLOWING THE NORTH-WEST
HIGHLAND TRACKS

THE proper way to follow a cross-country track is to seize upon a fine day and a rucksack, and be off, letting the road itself determine where to halt for the night. But this is a counsel of perfection, which the heavy advance bookings of Youth Hostels and Hotels during the summer make difficult to carry out. But in the bright spring weather of April or May, the hotels are not very likely to be full, and the gamble is worth the taking; and, of course, one can always be completely independent with a tent.

To fix a time-table and book accommodation in advance is something of a gamble on the weather, and for most people the best way is to explore the tracks from one or two fixed centres. By making full use of car, cycle or bus, it is often possible to explore the old trackways more pleasantly and less tiringly than by doggedly going from one end of a track to the other. I went over the Glen Affric-Kintail pass in two days, driving up Glen Affric from Cannich and then walking up to the head of the glen and Loch Affric; and making the twenty-mile circuit of the tracks of either side of Beinn Fhada on the second day; in both cases driving to and from Fort Augustus. The second trip makes a long day, for it is fifty miles to drive from Fort Augustus to Kintail, and the walk itself takes about eight hours, but it is a shorter day than going right through the pass in the one lap.

Mail buses, which meet the trains at the various stations on the Inverness-Wick and Inverness-Kyle of Lochalsh railway lines, provide a good transport service to the various villages in the North-West. From Lairg, these buses run up to Tongue, to Durness and Scourie via Overscaig, and to Lochinver via Oykell Bridge. From Garve, there is a mail bus to Ullapool and Achiltibuie (and on certain days a through bus from Inverness to Ullapool), and this connects with a small car to Dundonnell. From Achnasheen, a bus runs to Kinlochewe, Gairloch and Poolewe, and another to Torridon; from Strathcarron, there is a mail bus to Shieldaig on Loch Torridon.

These mail buses take the mail down in the morning to catch the southbound train, and wait for the northbound train and its mails and parcels, which they then bring back in the evening. They are usually of very little use to the walker when exploring trackways, as they usually seem to be going in the wrong direction at the wrong time, but they are very useful in getting to a particular centre. The Great Glen itself has a very good service of buses running from Fort William to Inverness, and these are very useful in reaching starting points or coming back in the evening after walking the tracks of the district.

Applecross and Glenelg are served by steamers from Kyle of Lochalsh and Mallaig. Neither place has a pier and one goes ashore in a small ferry-boat. In bad weather it is sometimes too rough for this to be done and the unfortunate passenger has to return whence he came and hope for a better day.

The North-West Highlands are fairly well covered by small hotels. The Reay Forest tracks in Sutherland are an exception, for the hotels at Overscaig, Scourie, Durness and Tongue are a very long way from the hills. From any of these places, a car is essential to reach the start of the hill tracks.

Southward, there are several hotels at Ullapool and a small inn at the other end of the track across from Ullapool to Oykell Bridge. This inn will drive one to one or other of the neighbouring hotels if it is already full up.

There are Youth Hostels at Tongue and Ullapool.

The Loch Maree-Kinlochewe country is well served with hotels (at Poolewe, Gairloch, Loch Maree, Kinlochewe) and Youth Hostels at Carn Dearg, Opinan, Craig and Inver Alligin (on Loch Torridon). Following the track south by the Coulin Pass, however, there is no inn between Kinlochewe and Struy in Strath Glass—a formidable gap—unless one could arrange for transport from Struy up the road to Loch Monar.

Strath Carron has several hotels and there are small temperance hotels at Applecross and Shieldaig.

Glen Affric has Cannich hotel at its foot, and Kintail Lodge at the other end of the track to Loch Duich. The two Youth Hostels at Ratagan and Buntait in Glen Urquhart are 37 miles apart which makes them rather unsuitable as bases for traversing the Glen Affric pass, much of which is certainly not easy walking.

The Great Glen has hotels at Invermoriston, Fort Augustus, Invergarry, Spean Bridge and Fort William; Youth Hostels at Alltsaigh (Loch Ness), Balalister, (Laggan, Loch Lochy), and Glen Nevis. Going westward to Kinlochhourn, there is an hotel at Tomdoun. On the Glenelg line by Glen Moriston, there is now no inn between Invermoriston and Kintail Lodge at the head of Loch Duich. Glenelg had a large hotel which, however, has been burned down; there is a Youth Hostel nearby at Kyle Rhea.

It is therefore quite practicable to walk the tracks from end to end, and by contacting some of the private houses on the routes, many of which take visitors, some of the distances could be considerably shortened. Most of the hotels have, of course, developed from inns along the line of important trackways and roads. They can be used either as stepping-stones along the road or as centres from which not only the trackways but the whole country through which they pass can be explored.

BIBLIOGRAPHY

THE following books and papers were among those consulted in writing *The Roads from the Isles*. They relate both to the roads themselves and to the country and its history through which the tracks pass. In many cases, they include further bibliographical lists.

Abbreviations: *P.S.A.S.* Proceedings of the Society of Antiquaries of Scotland.

Trans. I.F.C. Transactions of the Inverness Scientific Society and Field Club.

Trans. G.S.I. Transactions of the Gaelic Society of Inverness.

Mem. Geol. Surv. Memoirs of the Geological Survey, Scotland.

A Highland County Plans. Published by the County Council of Ross and Cromarty. Dingwall, 1947.

Blundell, Odo. "On Further Examination of Artificial Islands in the Beauly Firth, Loch Bruiach, Loch Moy, Loch Garry, Loch Lundy, Loch Oich, Loch Lochy and Loch Treig." *P.S.A.S.* Vol. 44, pp. 12-33.

"Notice of the Examination, by means of a Diving Dress, of the Artificial Island or Crannog of Eilean Muireach, in the South End of Loch Ness." *P.S.A.S.* Vol. 43, pp. 159-164.

"Further Notes on the Artificial Islands in the Highland area." *P.S.A.S.* Vol. 47, pp. 257-302.

Bogle, Lockhart. "Notes on some Prehistoric Structures in Glenelg and Kintail." *P.S.A.S.* Vol. 29, pp. 180-190.

Boswell's Journal of a Tour to the Hebrides with Samuel Johnson, LL.D. Published from the original manuscript, with notes by Frederick A. Pottle and Charles H. Bennett. London, 1936.

Cameron Lees, J. *County Histories of Scotland*. "Inverness." Edinburgh, 1897.

Childe, V. Gordon. *The Prehistory of Scotland*. London, 1935. *Scotland before the Scots*, being the Rhind lectures for 1944. London, 1946.

Childe, V. Gordon and Thorneycroft, Wallace. "The Experimental Production of the Phenomena Distinctive of Vitrified Forts." *P.S.A.S.* Vol. 72, pp. 44-55.

Chisholm, Colin. *The Clearance of the Highland Glens*. *Trans. G.S.I.* Vol. 6, pp. 174-188.

Curle, Alexander O. "An Account of the Ruins of the Broch of Dun Telve, near Glenelg, excavated by H.M. Office of Works in 1914." *P.S.A.S.* Vol. 50, pp. 241-254.
  "The Broch of Dun Troddan, Gleann Beag, Glenelg, Invernessshire." *P.S.A.S.* Vol. 55, pp. 83-94.

Dixon, J. H. *Gairloch*. Edinburgh, 1886.

Ellice, E. C. "Place Names of Glengarry and Glen Quoich and their Associations." 2nd Edition, London, 1931. "Invergarry Castle." *Trans. I.F.C.* Vol. 5, pp. 227-236.

Galbraith, J. J. "The Battle of Glenshiel, 1719." *Trans. G.S.I.* Vol. 34, pp. 280-313.

Grey, James. *Sutherland and Caithness in Saga-Time*. Edinburgh, 1922.

Historical Papers relating to the Jacobite Period, 1699-1750. Edited by Colonel James Allardyce. New Spalding Club, Aberdeen, 1896.

Inglis, Harry R. G. "The Roads and Bridges in the Early History of Scotland." *P.S.A.S.* Vol. 47, pp. 303-333.

Inverness and Dingwall Presbytery Records, 1643-1688. Edited by William MacKay. Scottish History Society, 1896.

Johnson, Samuel. *A Journey to the Western Isles*. First published 1775.

Ling, W. N. & Corbett, John Rooke. "The Northern Highlands." *Scottish Mountaineering Club Guide*. 2nd Edition, 1936.

Macadam. W. Iwison. "Notes on the Ancient Iron Industry of Scotland." *Trans. I.F.C.* Vol. 3, pp. 222-263.

MacDonald, Alexander. "Social Customs of the Gaels." Part 1, *Trans. G.S.I.* Vol. 32, pp. 272-301. Part 2, Vol. 33, pp. 122-146.

MacDonald, John. "The Highland Clearances." *Trans. G.S.I.* Vol. 1, pp. 79-85.

MacDonald, Kenneth. "A Modern Raid in Glengarry and Glen Moriston. The Burning of the Church of Cillechriost." *Trans. G.S.I.* Vol. 15, pp. 11-34.

MacBain, Alexander. *Place Names. The Highlands and Islands of Scotland.* Stirling, 1922.

MacFarlane, A. M. "Myths Associated with Mountains, Springs and Lochs in the Highlands." *Trans. G.S.I.* Vol. 34, pp. 135-152.

MacFarlane's Geographical Collections. Scottish History Society, 1906.

MacKay, William. "Three Unpublished Dispatches from General Monck." *Trans. G.S.I.* Vol. 18, pp. 70-78.

    Urquhart and Glen Moriston. Inverness, 1893.

    "An Inverness Merchant of the Olden Time." *Trans. G.S.I.* Vol. 23, pp. 281-309.

MacKenzie, Kenneth S. "Military Roads in the Highlands." *Trans. I.F.C.* Vol. 5, pp. 364-384.

MacKenzie, Osgood Hanbury. *A Hundred Years in the Highlands.* London, 1921.

Mem. Geol. Surv. "The Geological Structure of the North-West Highlands of Scotland." 1907.

    "The Geology of Central Sutherland." 1931.

    "The Geology of the Fannich Mountains." 1913.

    "The Geology of Glenelg, Lochalsh and South-East Part of Skye." 1910.

    "The Geology of the Country round Beauly and Inverness." 1914.

Murray, J. and Pullar, L. *Bathymetrical Survey of the Scottish Fresh Water Lochs.* Edinburgh, 1910.

Nairne, David. "Notes on Highland Woods, Ancient and Modern." *Trans. G.S.I.* Vol. 17, pp. 170-221.

New Statistical Account of Scotland. 1845. Vols. 14 (Ross and Cromarty: Inverness) and 15 (Sutherland).

Parker, James A. "The Western Highlands." *Scottish Mountaineering Club Guide.* Third Edition. 1947.

Pennant, Thomas. *A Tour of Scotland.* 3 vols. 1769-1772.

Phemister, J. *British Regional Geology. Scotland.* "The Northern Highlands." Edinburgh, 1936.

Reeves, William. "St. Maelrubha: His history and churches." *P.S.A.S.* Vol. 3, pp. 258-296.

Ritchie, James. "The Lake Dwelling or Crannog in Eadarloch, Loch Treig. Its Traditions and its Construction." *P.S.A.S.* Vol. 76, pp. 8-78.

Robertson, A. E. *Old Tracks, Cross-country Routes and "Coffin Roads" in the North-west Highlands.* Edinburgh, 1944.

Ross, Alexander. "The Caledonian Canal and its Effects on the Highlands." *Trans. G.S.I.* Vol. 13, pp. 313-335.

"Old Highland Industries." *Trans. G.S.I.* Vol. 12, pp. 387-415.

"Old Highland Roads." *Trans. G.S.I.* Vol. 14, pp. 172-193.

Salmond, J. B. *Wade in Scotland.* Edinburgh, 1938.

Scott, Archibald B. "The Brito-Celtic Church on the Northern Mainland and Islands." *Trans. G.S.I.* Vol. 33, pp. 327-355.

Scottish Forfeited Estates Papers. Scottish History Society. 1909.

Scrope, William. *Deer Stalking in the Scottish Highlands.* Glasgow, 1894.

Smith, W. A. *The Hill Paths, Drove Roads and "Cross Country" Routes in Scotland from the Cheviots to Sutherland.* Edinburgh, 1924.

Statistical Account of Scotland (Old). Vol. 3 (1792). Parishes of Durness, pp. 576-585; Gairloch, pp. 89-93 and Applecross, pp. 369-382. Vol. 6 (1793), Edderachylis, pp. 278-305 and Kintail, pp. 242-254. Vol. 7 (1793), Glenshiel, pp. 124-132. Vol. 10 (1794), Loch Broom, pp. 461-473. Vol. 11 (1794), Lochalsh, pp. 422-429. Vol. 16 (1795), Assynt, pp. 163-211 and Glenelg, pp. 265-274.

Sutherland and the Reay Country. Edited by Adam Gunn and John MacKay. Glasgow, 1897.

The Lyon in Mourning. Scottish History Society. 3 vols. 1895.

Wallace, T.D. "Military Roads and Fortifications in the Highlands, with Bridges and Milestones." *P.S.A.S.* Vol. 45, pp. 318-333.

"Notes of Antiquities in Loch Alsh and Kintail." *P.S.A.S.* Vol. 31, pp. 68-89.

Watson, W. J. *History of the Celtic Place Names of Scotland.* The Rhind lectures for 1916. Edinburgh, 1926.

INDEX OF PLACE NAMES